SIR WALTER RALEIGH

Raleigh the Favourite

A Miniature of Raleigh—the reproduction is the actual size—on his first coming to court in 1582. His head-dress, it will be noticed, is in the French fashion which was popular at the moment in deference to the Duke of Anjou who was wooing the Queen

SIR
WALTER RALEIGH

★

HUGH
ROSS WILLIAMSON

GREENWOOD PRESS, PUBLISHERS
WESTPORT, CONNECTICUT

Library of Congress Cataloging in Publication Data

Ross Williamson, Hugh, 1901-
   Sir Walter Raleigh.

   Reprint of the 1951 ed. published by Faber and
Faber, London.
   Includes index.
   1. Raleigh, Walter, Sir, 1552?-1618. 2. Great
Britain--History--Elizabeth, 1558-1603. 3. Great
Britain--History--James I, 1603-1625. 4. Explorers--
England--Biography. 5. Great Britain--Court and
courtiers--Biography.
DA86.22.R2R6 1978   942.05'5'0924 [B]   78-17033
ISBN 0-313-20577-9

First published in mcmli

Reprinted with the permission of Margaret Ross-Williamson

Reprinted in 1978 by Greenwood Press, Inc.
51 Riverside Avenue, Westport, CT. 06880

Printed in the United States of America

10 9 8 7 6 5 4 3 2 1

EPISTLE DEDICATORY
TO MY GOD-SON, JEREMY SHAW

My dear Jeremy,

I have tried to write you this short life of one of the greatest Englishmen of all time that you may know enough about him to want to know more. If it sends you to longer and more detailed biographies, such as those written by Milton Waldman and Edward Thompson, I shall feel that it has achieved its purpose. You may even care to go on, behind these fairly recent 'lives', to some of the older writers and one day, I hope—if you take up history seriously—to the sources themselves.

In case you do, there are one or two warnings I feel I must give you. You must remember that Raleigh was a much-hated man and there have always been those, from his own lifetime till to-day, who, because of their enmity to him, have denied his greatness. You will find this among some who are reckoned great historians and the reason for their dislike seems to be that they spent most of their academic life in producing books about Raleigh's enemies. Gardiner, for instance, tried to whitewash King James I and Spedding found a hero in Francis Bacon. When you know the period, you will understand that nothing more need be said.

As for the eighteenth-century writer, Hume, who started the modern fashion of attacking Raleigh, I can do no better than quote to you von Hügel's words to his god-daughter when, in unforgettable indignation, he asked her why she should want to waste her time reading Hume: 'Hume is blasé. He is the sort of person young people are taken in by; they take him for something else. He knows everything. . . . If I were to die to-night, he would know all about me by to-morrow. These old bones would all be arranged, sorted out, explained and in his coat pocket; but somehow he would not have got me, all the same.' Hume, in fact, is as starkly incapable of comprehending Raleigh as are apologists for King James or Francis Bacon.

I do not mean, of course, that Raleigh had not great faults. In his younger days he was ruthless and cruel. Almost to the end, he was arrogant and inconsiderate. But he knew it and repented it, and in his last prayer on the scaffold he acknowledged it and explained it almost in the same breath. 'Join with me', he asked the bystanders, 'in prayer to that great God of Heaven whom I have grievously offended, being a man full of all vanity, who has lived a sinful life in such callings as have been most inducing to it. I have been a seafaring man, a soldier and a courtier, and in the temptations of the least of these there is enough to overthrow a good mind and a good man.'

But Raleigh was more than a sailor, a soldier and a courtier. He was also a great poet and a great historian, a scientist, a philosopher, an explorer and an administrator. This, indeed, is the measure of his greatness, for the essential of any true greatness is this kind of versatility. The little man is one 'who can only achieve selfhood by concentrating on a narrow selection of interests'. Such a man may indeed be—in fact, usually is—a successful man, simply because he does so concentrate. He may rise—he usually does—to high and important places. But he remains a little man all the same.

As you read this story, you will find many such men in the ranks of Raleigh's enemies. Do not be surprised that they include kings and eminent lawyers and millionaires and high ecclesiastics and powerful statesmen. There is one more lesson that you cannot learn too young—that implied by the question of a great Swedish statesman (a contemporary of Raleigh) to his son: 'Doest thou not know, my son, with how little wisdom the world is governed?' You will find in this book something about men governing and how their victim, Raleigh, still stands towering above them all.

Because I am writing to you, there is one other thing I must say. It concerns Raleigh's attitude to Christianity (which, for us, is what all men must finally be judged by). He was called an atheist and a blasphemer by the Protestants. To the Catholics, he was not only a heretic, but a heretic who was an active enemy of the Faith. But there is this to be remembered. He had been brought up in complete ignorance of what the Catholic Faith was. All he knew was fantastic propaganda inaccuracies about the 'mumbo-jumbo' religion of England's national enemy, Spain. When he turned to the religion in which he had been brought up—the Protestantism which was, so to speak, part of his patriotism—he was taught two things. One was that 'the Bible and the Bible alone is the religion of Protestants', and the other that every man had a right of private judgment in religious matters. So he applied his mind—a subtle, questioning mind—to exercising his private judgment on what the Bible was and so horrified his co-religionists that they considered him almost the Devil himself.

So, in his own day, he found himself at odds with all the religion he knew, though in the end, through adversities and prayer, he managed to fight his way through to a great and certain faith.

Your affectionate god-father,

HUGH ROSS WILLIAMSON

London,
Epiphany, 1951

CONTENTS

CONTENTS

ILLUSTRATIONS

PLATES

IN THE TEXT

CHAPTER ONE

BEGINNINGS

Whereas Queen Elizabeth came to the throne of
England in 1558, Walter Raleigh was a six-
year-old boy, living in his father's house at
Hayes Barton near Budleigh Salterton in Devon. Among
his relatives were men whose names were to become
famous in the new reign as explorers, adventurers, col-
onizers, sea-fighters and pirates. Looking back on it now,
we can see that he was at the heart of much of what we
mean when we speak of 'the Elizabethan Age' and which
a song expresses by saying that whenever Queen Elizabeth was in trouble she sent for a Devon man. But it did
not mean that to him at the time. He was only the youngest son of a country squire, not particularly important or
wealthy, far away from the great world, where men were
famous or fortunate. The prizes were there for the win-
ning—but not in Devon. They were in London, at Court
or in the city, and beyond the sea, in discovery or in
warfare. Walter Raleigh, when he grew up, was to gain
them all and to find out how much they were worth; but
even when he was the most powerful man in England he
never quite lost the spirit of the country boy, dreaming of
splendour a long way away.

From his boyhood, too, he knew that nothing could be
won without fighting. That, in the little world he lived

in, was taken for granted. Personal courage and skill in swordsmanship were among the first necessities. Here too he was to learn of other ways in which the fight for power was conducted in the great world where the tongue could be more deadly than the sword and where money could outfight both. Again, though from time to time he was to use other weapons, he kept that kind of boyish courage which, because of its simplicity, is often cruel, though in a way quite distinct from the complicated cruelty of the coward. Also, like a boy, he fought to win and he fought for his own hand.

Of his undergraduate days at Oriel College, Oxford, only two stories have come down to us. One is the conventional circumstance that he once borrowed a gown and forgot to return it, but the other is already individual. A fellow undergraduate, who was a coward but a good archer, asked Raleigh's advice as to how best to gain satisfaction for an insult. Raleigh told him to challenge his opponent to a shooting match at the butts.

All that we know certainly of his youth is concerned with fighting. What kind of education he had at Hayes Barton we can only guess. It was probably what he picked up at home—all his life he remained an excited reader of everything he could lay hands on—but it was good enough to provoke this judgment on him in his teens at Oxford: 'His natural parts being strangely advanced by academic learning, he became the ornament of the juniors and was worthily esteemed a proficient in oratory and philosophy.' The surrounding atmosphere of his family, however, we do know. His uncle, Sir Arthur Champernoun, was Vice-Admiral of the West, commanding at Plymouth; his half-brother, Humphrey Gilbert, thirteen years his senior, was already known as a dour and terrible soldier; Francis Drake was a cousin of his father's first wife; Richard Grenville, perhaps the wildest of them all, was his own cousin. Altogether Raleigh was able to count 'more than a hundred gentlemen of my kindred'—the Carews and the Courtenays, the St. Legers and the Russels among them—who formed, as it were, a fighting border clan; and when he was only sixteen it was for soldiering in France, under one of the Champernoun cousins, that he deserted Oxford to learn the realities of warfare.

The civil war in France was, in name at least, a religious struggle between Catholics and Huguenots. As the Devon clan was Protestant, it was natural that they should fight on the Huguenot side; yet, in a sense, their intervention in the warfare was a family matter, for Champernoun was the son-in-law of the Huguenot leader, Montgomeri. In France, Raleigh, as one of the hundred Devon volunteers, was at the battles of Montcontour and Jarnac. It is possible (though, some historians think, not probable) that he was among the crowd of refugees in the English Embassy in Paris on the night of the massacre of St. Bartholomew. It is certain that he watched the Huguenots smoking out a band of their enemies in the caves of Languedoc, for he has left us a description of it: 'We knew not how to enter by any ladder or engine, till at last, by certain bundles of lighted straw let down by an iron chain with a weighty stone in the midst, those that defended it were so smothered that they surrendered themselves, with their plate, money and other goods therein hidden; or they must have died like bees that are smoked out of their hives.'

BEGINNINGS

Raleigh's apprenticeship to the school of life was thus served in this bitter civil war whose realities were bloodshed and plunder, hatred and 'no quarter' and it left its mark on him. It gave to his courage an edge of ruthlessness which it was never to lose. It made him see civil war as an evil by which no nation's condition was ever bettered. And it fed a kind of contempt for religion in the name of which such things as he had seen could be done. Charges made against him in later years—his atrocities in Ireland, his relentlessness in the Essex rebellion, his atheism—must, at the bar of history, take account of the effects on him of this early schooling.

He returned from France, probably, at the end of 1574. In his absence, his name had remained on the register of his university and, in the February of 1575, he was entered as a Member of the Middle Temple. His career was following the usual course for young men of his kind. Members of the squirearchy had to have some knowledge of law, though whether Raleigh ever regarded the Inns of Court as anything much more than a London club is open to doubt. During this time—from 1575 to 1577—he lived at Islington and, again, what knowledge we have of him mainly consists of stories of his wildness. On one occasion, becoming annoyed with a bore, whose voice went on and on 'like a drum in a room', he stopped his mouth by fastening his moustaches to his beard with sealing-wax. On another, he had to bail out two of his servants for assaulting a watchman. And he himself was hauled before the Privy Council and sentenced to a week's imprisonment in the Fleet for duelling.

Among the 'boisterous blades' who were his chief companions was George Gascoigne, the poet who wrote the second earliest blank verse tragedy in English and the earliest critical essay. Gascoigne was a friend of Raleigh's half-brother, now Sir Humphrey Gilbert, and had served with him in the wars in Flanders. On their return in 1576, Gascoigne published a new poem entitled *The Steel Glass* and bound up with it were polite prefatory verses by young Raleigh. Though they were not particularly good verses, they contained one couplet which might have stood as Raleigh's warning to himself:

> *For whoso reaps renown above the rest*
> *With heaps of hate shall surely be oppressed.*

But the days when Raleigh was to be the most renowned and, because of it, the best hated man in England were still in the future. At the moment he was still confined to a little world. Though he could take a place on the fringes of the Court, he was unnoticed among the great throng striving for a place there; and neither his sword nor his personality nor his poetry (and poetry, in the Elizabethan Court, was also a weapon) could take him to the centre. Had Gascoigne lived, that patronage might have helped him on; but the poet died in 1577, leaving Raleigh nothing but his motto: *Tam Marti quam Mercurio*, which Raleigh thereupon adopted as his own to announce his double nature as soldier and scholar.

He turned his gaze to another part of the horizon. For years Sir Humphrey Gilbert had been pestering the Privy Council to allow him to found a colony in the New World. Some of his schemes were too vague or too dangerous for any notice to be taken of them, but when he submitted a proposal to confine his activities to 'the northern part of America ... inhabited by a savage people

19

of a mild and tractable disposition' as 'of all other un-
frequented places the one most fitted and most com-
modious for us to meddle with', the Council in the June
of 1578 granted him a patent to discover and annex 'any
remote, barbarous and heathen lands not possessed by any
Christian prince or people'. Raleigh, naturally, joined his
half-brother in the scheme. Here at last it seemed, was a
certain way to fame and fortune.

It did not turn out like that. The little fleet which set
out in the September of 1578 was driven back by the
autumn storms into Plymouth. It set out again in November, this time to meet the Spaniards who attacked it off
Cape Verde and inflicted much damage. Each ship found
its way back as best it could. Last of all came Raleigh, in
command of the *Falcon*, with the motto *Nec mortem peto
nec finem fugio* (I neither seek death nor flee the end). The
weather, the Spaniards and the lack of provisions had
beaten even his grim determination to go on.

He was twenty-seven, back at Hayes Barton, a failure.

CHAPTER TWO

CAPTAIN IN IRELAND

Ireland was on the verge of rebellion. For years there had been smouldering hostilities, as the Irish tried to drive out the English colonists who, seeking their fortune there, regarded the natives somewhat in the light of vermin to be exterminated. Hatred was brought to a head by Elizabeth's attempt to force Protestantism on Catholic Ireland, so that the struggle became, as in France, complicated by the religious issue. The Catholic powers on the Continent gave some little aid to their co-religionists. In 1579, a small expedition having the authority of the Pope landed at Dingle, but was soon defeated. In 1580, a larger number of Italians and Spaniards landed at Smerwick. And the Earl of Desmond rose in a rebellion in Munster which was not crushed till 1583.

It was to this Ireland that Raleigh now volunteered to go. As captain of a band of a hundred soldiers, he landed there in the August of 1580 and was immediately commissioned, with one of his St. Leger cousins, to try the brother of the Earl of Desmond, who had fallen into English hands. The Irish leader was immediately hanged, drawn and quartered.

As Raleigh began, so he proceeded. He was responsible, in November, for the massacre at Smerwick. The Spaniards who had landed and were besieged there, with many

of the Irish, had after many attempts to parley surrendered
and begged for mercy. Lord Grey, the Deputy of Ireland,
sent Raleigh into the fort. Raleigh ordered a general massacre of men and women, foreigners and Irish alike. About
six hundred stripped bodies—'as gallant and goodly per-
sonages as ever were beheld', according to Lord Grey—
were laid out on the sands.

'It is horrible to remember Raleigh in Ireland; it is
horrible to remember *any* Elizabethan in Ireland', one of
Raleigh's biographers has written. We may leave it at
that, not attempting to excuse the inexcusable. At the
same time, it must be recorded that Raleigh left also the
legend of his courage, differing in this, if not in pitiless-
ness, from his companions.

On one occasion, he was riding ahead of his company
with a guide when he was ambushed at a ford. He managed to fight his own way through but, on gaining the
further bank of the river, turned and saw that his companion had been thrown from his horse and was strug-
gling desperately in mid-stream. He dashed back and with
pistol and quarter-staff held off the twenty ambushers
until the main body of his men came up and the attackers
fled.

His most famous exploit was the capture of Lord Roche,
an Anglo-Irish nobleman who was suspected of dis-
loyalty. At the head of ninety men, he made a forced
march at night through dangerous country. Arriving at
dawn, he disposed his band secretly about the castle where
five hundred were prepared for resistance and, with only
six companions, demanded a parley. Roche eventually
gave him permission to enter with two companions. He
accepted but, by a ruse of which we have no exact record,

managed to smuggle the whole of his company into the castle. Though still hopelessly outnumbered, he immobilized his opponents by threatening to kill Lord Roche immediately if any move were made to rescue him and took him under arrest to Cork. This involved once more a forced march at night in torrential rain over difficult country which was now ambushed by intending rescuers, one band of them eight hundred strong. The march was so terrible that one man actually dropped dead from exhaustion, but Raleigh's will accomplished the apparently impossible and the prisoner was delivered safely.

Yet for all his bravery and brilliance, Raleigh was unpopular with his superiors. The Deputy, Lord Grey, admitted frankly: 'I like neither his carriage nor his company,' and Raleigh, on his part, eventually wrote to the Earl of Leicester, the powerful favourite of the Queen who had procured him his command: 'I have spent some time here under the Deputy in such poor place and charge as, were it not that I know him to be one of yours, I would disdain it as much as to keep sheep.'

In addition to a personal dislike, there was a disagreement on policy. On the one hand, Raleigh considered Grey a feeble and incompetent governor. If one was fighting a rebellion, there was only one immediate object —to crush it. Grey's rule had ensured anything but this. Writing to the Secretary of State, Walsingham, Raleigh remarked bitterly: 'There are at this instant a thousand traitors more than there were the first day.' On the other hand, Raleigh considered that Grey's policy, such as it was, lacked discrimination. He urged that it would be wise to try to win over the smaller Irish chieftains, who were weary of expense and violence and who were afraid that the English would eventually make peace with Desmond and leave them victims to clan vengeance.

On both counts Raleigh was obviously right. But his endeavour to undermine Grey by appealing over his head —or, more exactly, behind his back—to Grey's superiors in England raises other questions. By modern standards, this would be accounted flagrantly disloyal, but, though Grey himself naturally denounced it, it was conventional Elizabethan conduct. The etiquette of the civil service had not then been invented. Also, and more importantly, it reveals a dominant characteristic of Raleigh—his impatience of mediocrity. He had what was probably one of the most brilliant and certainly the most versatile of minds in even that amazing age. As a poet, he was to challenge comparison with the greatest, Shakespeare only excepted; as an adventurer, colonizer and sea-fighter, he was greater than Drake; as scientist and philosopher, he overshadowed Bacon; in statecraft, he was as shrewd as Cecil; as an historian, on the one hand, and as a public figure on the other, he had no equal at all. Such a many-sided genius, living, as it were, half a dozen lives, was inevitably out of tune with the slow-moving, plodding temperament essential to those who seek success only in one groove. His mercurial swiftness of mind, which enabled him to see in an instant what others only slowly comprehended, made him impatient even of his equals and intolerant of his intellectual inferiors. When such an inferior was, like Grey, in command not because of his ability, but because of his birth and background, Raleigh's rage and frustration could not be contained. Nor, to the end of his life, did he ever master the first lesson of successful diplomacy—the art not only of suffering fools gladly but when appropriate allowing oneself to appear an even greater fool.

In another way, too, his attack on his superior was characteristic of him. He had taken service in Ireland for no reason but to make his way and his fortune. It was quite clear that Grey would not aid him in this. If he was to be noticed in London, it would have to be by his own action. And, quite unscrupulously, he took it.

He was successful. In the December of 1581, his company was disbanded and he was sent to England with despatches to the Privy Council. Here, according to one version of the story, he had a personal altercation with Grey, 'where he had much the better in telling of his tale; and so much that the Queen and the Lords took no small mark of the man and his parts.'

Whatever the exact circumstances of the meeting, the result was soon obvious to everybody. The Queen 'took him for a kind of oracle, which nettled them all'.

CHAPTER THREE

THE COURTIER

The two famous stories of how Raleigh won his
way into Elizabeth's favour may not be true. He
may never have taken off his cloak and laid it in
'a plashy place' for her to tread on. He may never have
written with a diamond on a window:

> *Fain would I climb*
> *Yet I fear to fall*

for her to answer with:

> *If thy heart fail thee*
> *Climb not at all.*

But these episodes are certainly in character. If they did
not happen, they ought to have happened. They are in the
true Raleighan tradition. The obscure soldier from Ireland, finding himself at last at the heart of the glittering
Court, where theatrical flamboyance, fantastic make-
believe and poetic love-making were the order of the day,
had come into his own. What for others was deliberate
affectation was for him natural and spontaneous—part of
his *panache*. At a deeper level, the restless vitality of his
mind matched the Queen's; and it is a tribute to them
both that, in spite of periods of disgrace and the ascendancy of other favourites, Raleigh and the Queen

remained faithful to each other, in their fashion, until
Elizabeth's death, twenty-one years later.

The moment of his arrival coincided with the last
months of the visit of the Duke of Anjou, the French
king's brother, with whom Elizabeth, for diplomatic
reasons, was carrying on marriage negotiations. Masques
and dances, banquets and tournaments were the order of
the day. Outwardly, splendour was at its most splendid.
But in fact no one, with the possible exception of Anjou,
took the marriage project seriously, though everyone had
to pretend to. Its political importance was that, because of
Anjou's claim to the Netherlands, Elizabeth could use
him in the diplomatic struggle against Spain. When, in
the February of 1582, he left for the Low Countries to be
invested as Duke of Brabant, the Queen herself went with
him as far as Canterbury and on parting protested that she
lived only for his prompt return, urging him to write to
her every day as his wife. On the voyage the Duke was
accompanied by the Earl of Leicester, who carried Elizabeth's secret instructions to the Prince of Orange to keep
Anjou in Holland at any cost and never let him come
back to England. In Leicester's train of nobles and gentlemen went Walter Raleigh. As part of his duty was to
establish a personal contact with the Prince of Orange,
and as he remained for a short time in Holland after
Leicester's return to England, it is possible, even probable, that Raleigh was in the secret and thus gained his
first insight into diplomacy at the highest level.

It was not long before Raleigh was back in London to
astonish everyone by his meteoric rise. The two dominant
figures of the Court were Leicester and Burleigh—
Leicester, who had grown up with Elizabeth and who

was so enduringly powerful in her affections that many believed that she was secretly married to him; and Burleigh, the wise statesman and architect of Elizabethen policy whom she trusted as surely as she loved Leicester. The reigning favourite was an inconsiderable little man, Sir Christopher Hatton, whose skill in dancing had brought him to her notice—one who 'came to the Court by the galliard, a mere vegetable of the Court that sprung up at night'.

Elizabeth called him her 'skipping sheep'. Such royal nicknames were the order of the day. Burleigh was her 'spirit', Leicester, her 'eyes'; Anjou (who was small and a hunchback) had been her 'frog'; Raleigh, because of his sea-faring background and the usual pronunciation of his Christian name, became, obviously enough, 'water'. Later, he improved it in a typically grandiose fashion to 'ocean', in which form it still lives in English literature, both in his own great poem to the Queen: *The Ocean's Love to Cynthia* and in the title of his friend and protégé, Edmund Spenser, 'the Shepherd of the Ocean'. At the moment, however, the Court preferred to think of him merely as a bucket.

One morning when the Queen was riding in the park a friend of Hatton's suddenly stepped out of a thicket where he had been hiding and presented her with a letter, a little silver bucket and a jewelled bodkin. The meaning of this, as the letter explained, was that her sheep would kill himself unless the water was removed. Elizabeth replied that she would allow no single element so to abound as to breed confusion and that her sheep 'was so dear unto her, that she had bounded her banks so sure, as no *water* nor floods should ever overthrow them'. She sent Hatton, in return, a little silver dove—'a bird that, together with the rainbow, brought the good tidings that there should be no more destruction by water'. Hatton was not altogether reassured and his friends' comment that 'water hath been more welcome than were fit for so cold a season' accurately expressed the real situation. Nothing, at that moment, could stem the rising tide of Raleigh's favour, and by 1583 he was in so strong a position that even Burleigh asked him to use his influence with the Queen to intercede for his son-in-law, the Earl of Oxford, who had been duelling.

As the years passed the favours increased, as may be seen from a mere chronicle of them. In 1583, he was granted the farm of wines, which meant in practice that he had the right to collect £1 a year from every vintner in the country. The same year the Queen gave him the use of Durham House in the Strand, where he kept forty men and horses in attendance on him and used as his study 'a little turret that looked into and over the Thames and had a prospect which is as pleasant as any in the world'. In 1584 he was granted the monopoly of the export of woollen broadcloth—more lucrative even than the wine licence—was knighted and became Member of Parliament for Devonshire. In 1585 he was made Lord Warden of the Stanneries, that is to say, governor of the Devon and Cornwall tin-miners, a community of about 13,000, with laws of its own. Against this appointment, a protest was made to Burleigh that 'no man is more hated than him; none more cursed daily of the poor, of whom in truth numbers are brought to extreme poverty through the gift of the cloths to him; his pride is intolerable, without regard for any, as the world knows', but in spite of this he was given, in addition to the Wardenship, the Lieutenancy of the County of Cornwall and Vice-Admiralship of Devon and Cornwall. In 1586 he was granted vast estates in five Midland counties and more than forty thousand acres in Ireland, as a belated reward for his earlier service there. And in 1587 he gained the highest prize of all. He was made Captain of the Queen's Guard, which was not only the stepping-stone to the highest offices of State but was the coveted post which kept the occupant always near the Queen, with right of access to her at all times.

Such was Raleigh at thirty-five, 'the best hated man of the world, in Court, city and country'—and the most remarkable. Six feet tall, with a swarthy complexion, long, melancholy face, pointed beard and heavily-lidded eyes, he outdistanced every fashion. His jewelled shoes were said to be worth more than 6,600 gold pieces, his hat-band of pearls, his ear-rings, the silks and damasks he wore and the ornaments with which he bedecked himself were worth a king's ransom. And he had the pride of the peacock he appeared. In his Devonshire accent (which always amused Elizabeth and which he kept all his life) he would utter witticisms that wounded and insults none dared challenge. He knew what men said of him, but treated it with contempt. 'If any man accuseth me to my face, I will answer him with my mouth, but my tail is good enough to return an answer to such who traduceth me behind my back.' The ballad-mongers sang:

> Raleigh doth time bestride,
> He sits 'twixt wind and time,
> Yet uphill he cannot ride,

THE COURTIER

For all his bloody pride . . .
He seeks taxes in the tin,
He polls the poor to the skin,
Yet he vows 'tis no sin,
Lord, for thy pity!

This might seem nothing but the hate of envy. There was nothing to prevent him riding as high as he wished. Or so it seemed. Yet they were right. In 1587 the newly appointed Captain of the Guard discovered a rival. The young Earl of Essex came to Court.

CHAPTER FOUR

NEWFOUNDLAND AND VIRGINIA

Duringthose five years of unchallenged ascendancy, Raleigh was, nevertheless, the Queen's prisoner. He was given everything but permission to leave Court. She would not allow him even to return to Ireland. Still less would she let him go adventuring in the New World. Yet that is where his dreams led him and it was on such adventure, by proxy, that he spent much of his fortune.

Sir Humphrey Gilbert, so impoverished by his earlier ill luck that he had, so he said, been forced 'to sell his wife's clothes from her back', was begging to be allowed to make one more attempt at colonization. Raleigh pleaded his brother's case, begged to be allowed to go with him as Vice-Admiral and spent £2,000 in building a ship for the expedition, the *Bark Raleigh*.[1] At last, in the March of 1583, the Queen consented to allow Gilbert to sail, but was adamant that Raleigh himself must remain at home.

'Brother,' wrote Raleigh to Gilbert, announcing the news, 'I have sent you a token from Her Majesty, an anchor guided by a lady, as you see; and farther, Her Highness willed me to send you word that she wished you

[1] Not to be confused with his later *Ark Raleigh*, Lord Howard's flagship against the Armada.

as great good hap, and safety to your ship, as if her self were there in person; desiring you to have care of yourself, as of that which she tendereth; and therefore for her sake you must provide for it accordingly. Further, she commandeth me that you leave your picture with me. For the rest, I leave till our meeting, or to the report of this bearer, who would needs be messenger of this good news. So I commit you to the will and protection of God, Who sends us such life or death as He shall please or hath appointed.—Your true brother, W. RALEIGH.'

In June, five vessels—of which the *Bark Raleigh* was half the total tonnage—set out from Plymouth, carrying men for the projected colony, as well as 'morris dancers, Hobby horses and Maylike conceits to delight the savage people'. On the second day out, after encountering a fierce thunderstorm, the *Bark Raleigh* fled back to port. The excuse the commander of it gave was that a contagious sickness had broken out among the crew; but Gilbert himself, disbelieving, wrote: 'I pray you, solicit my brother Raleigh to make them an example to all knaves.'

With the other four ships Gilbert reached Newfoundland safely, annexed it and left colonists there. In August he sent the sick back to England and then, with the *Delight*, the *Golden Hind* and the tiny *Squirrel* (which he used as his flagship) continued the voyage in search of the fabled North-West Passage. They ran into fogs and wind and ice. They heard 'strange voices' in the night, 'which scared some from the helm'. The *Delight* ran aground and was dashed to pieces by the waves, only twelve of her crew of over a hundred escaping with their lives. But still the other two ships went on, cruising along the unknown coast, until the men, starving and in rags, were in such

c   33

plight that Gilbert at last consented to return. 'Be content,' he said, 'we have seen enough and take no care of expense past. I will set you forth royally the next Spring, if God send us safe home.' Somehow they reached the Azores, where they ran into a tempest. Gilbert, in spite of entreaties, refused to leave the *Squirrel*: 'I will not forsake my little company going homeward, with whom I have passed so many storms and perils.' And the last glimpse of him which the men in the *Golden Hind* had, before the sea took him, was 'sitting abaft with a book in his hand' calmly reiterating: 'We are as near to Heaven by sea as by land.'

Within seven months of his half-brother's death, Raleigh himself obtained from the Queen a patent similar to that which had been granted to Gilbert, authorizing him to plant a colony in the New World. Once again, he himself was not permitted to go, but as architect and financier of the project, he sent out, in the April of 1584, a small expedition to prospect for a suitable site. The explorers landed on and in the Queen's name took possession of what is now the island of Wokoken, off the coast of North Carolina. 'Wingandacoa!' was the response of the natives to the white men's questions, but according to Raleigh, this merely meant: 'You wear good clothes!' On the other hand, it may have been the island's name derived from that of its prince, Wingina. In any case, it was not altogether unlike Virginia, which Elizabeth allowed it to be called in her honour when the prospectors returned with specimens of skins, pearls and the native population.

The success of the prospectors led to the preparation of a larger expedition. In the April of 1585, ten vessels set out

under the command of Raleigh's cousin, Sir Richard
Grenville, and inaugurated the first English colony of 107
settlers under Governor Ralph Lane. The story of the
vicissitudes of Virginia—a land which its founder never
saw—does not properly belong to the picture of Raleigh.
It is only a far background, from which emerged certain
consequences. In brief, it was a story of failure and mis-
management. The settlers quarrelled among themselves,
fell foul of the Indians, ran short of food and, when Drake
called at the island the following spring, thankfully accepted his offer of a passage home. When Grenville returned with relief, he found them gone; but he left fifteen
new men to hold the fort till a fresh expedition could be
sent. This expedition Raleigh despatched in 1587 under
Captain John White and twelve picked lieutenants as 'the
Governor and assistants of the City of Raleigh in Virginia', but when they arrived they found that the temporary garrison had disappeared without trace. They
themselves eventually suffered the same fate and in 1589
Raleigh, having spent a fortune in his abortive effort to
found an empire, sold his patent.

It is idle to speculate whether, had the Queen allowed
him to cross the Atlantic himself, the project would have
been successful; but it is at least certain that his own plans
were not followed and that the spirit of Grenville, with
that streak of cruelty and instability which amounted at
times almost to madness, was far different from his own.
Grenville's temperament was nearer to Drake's—a pirate
and a destroyer—than to Raleigh's, which, though ruthless and greedy enough of gold, was also that of a builder
and a statesman.

The obvious temptation to all the English adventurers

of the time was to turn from the slow labours of colonization to the quick profits of piracy. It was easier, as well as
more exciting, to plunder the Spanish ships of their accu-
mulated treasures than to discover and work new sources
of wealth; and there was no international law in the matter which was likely to disturb Elizabeth. On his first
return journey from Virginia, Grenville, on an impro-
vised raft which sank as he reached his prize, boarded a
large Spanish ship laden with gold, silver, pearls, cochineal, sugar, ivory and hides, which he took as booty.
Raleigh—since it was 'Raleigh's expedition'—bore the
blame for it in Spain, without any counterbalancing gain,
since, when the treasure arrived in England, the Queen
seized it 'without so much as even giving him one pearl'.
As a further result, he incurred the hatred of the Stukeley
family, who considered that, as a Stukeley had been one
of those who helped to capture it, they were entitled to a
share of it. And it was the younger Stukeley, nursing revenge, who was to be the 'Judas' who eventually betrayed
Raleigh to death.

Besides Grenville and Stukeley, there is one other name
in the Virginia expedition which is to reappear throughout Raleigh's life—that of Thomas Harriot. In 1580, Raleigh, at a time when he himself had very little money,
took Harriot, then a young man of twenty, into his house
as mathematical tutor. It was the beginning of a friendship which was to last till Raleigh's death, and Harriot
was with him the night before his execution. Harriot was
to become one of the greatest scientists of the century. He
was ahead of Galileo in his use of the telescope, in which
he used 'especially to see Venus horned like the Moon and
the spots in the Sun', and he made a precise observance of

Halley's Comet in 1609. As a mathematician, his discoveries in algebra and pure mathematics were far in advance of his age, though, as he refused to publish during his lifetime, others subsequently gained credit for what were in fact his discoveries. He corresponded with Kepler. From him Descartes himself is said to have learned.

Now, at the age of twenty-five, he went to Virginia as Raleigh's eyes and returned, with the little band brought home by Drake, to publish in *A Brief and True Report of the Land of Virginia* a survey of the crops, merchandise, flora, fauna and minerals of the country to which nothing comparable in systematic method and precision had been produced by any explorer.

Among other things, in this book, he made strong claims for the habit of smoking, the medicinal virtues of which 'would require a column to relate' and which Raleigh consequently endeavoured to popularize in England. The discovery of tobacco was now added to the growing Raleigh legend. The story of how his servant, seeing smoke issuing from his mouth, imagined him on fire and threw a bucket of water over him may be apocryphal, but from this date no imagined picture of him is complete without his long silver pipe and gold tobacco-case, which, no less than his jewelled shoes and daggered tongue, became a ground of wonder and offence.

So Virginia and what was to prove its most important product, Virginia tobacco, invaded the Court where he flashed his way through its artificial intricacies while, far away, his expeditions foundered and failed. One day, he bragged to the Queen that he understood tobacco so well that he could even tell what the smoke weighed. Elizabeth challenged him with a wager. Raleigh accepted, weighed a quantity of tobacco, smoked it and then weighed the ashes. The Queen, who had expected an easy victory, did not deny 'what was wanting in the prime weight of the tobacco to have been evaporated in smoke', but paid her losses with the remark that 'many labourers in the fire she had heard of who turned their gold into smoke, but Raleigh was the first who had turned smoke into gold'.

CHAPTER FIVE

ESSEX

In the little world of the Court there was less immediate interest in the discovery of foreign lands than in
the arrival of a new favourite, and Robert Devereux,
Earl of Essex, was a personage who kept and held men's
attention—and the Queen's. He was her cousin, Leicester's
step-son, Burleigh's ward. The centre of the Court was,
thus, his natural place and he brought to it not only a
handsome presence and a personality which could sway
crowds as well as individuals, but some of the oldest blood
in England. His ancestry could be traced back directly to
Edward III, but he was descended also from most of the
great medieval houses who had intermarried with the
Royal House. Besides him most of Elizabeth's Court—
even Leicester, certainly Burleigh—were parvenus. He
might be the poorest earl in England, but he was among
the most certain aristocrats.

This circumstance was of relevance to his dealings with
Raleigh, the obscure Devon gentleman. Their relative
status was immediately understood by both of them.
Moreover, the twenty-year-old Essex spoke to the Queen,
as if by right, in tones that the thirty-five-year-old Raleigh, for all his pride of place, would never dare use. And
in their first recorded clash—it was the summer of 1587—
the situation was perfectly defined.

Throughout the spring days the Queen had had 'nobody near her but my Lord of Essex; and at night my Lord is at cards, or one game or another, with her till the birds sing in the morning', but Raleigh remained officially in favour. It was when the Court went on its summer Progress that antagonism became defined and unconcealed. At Lord Warwick's, among the other guests, was a friend of Lady Warwick, Essex's sister, Lady Perrott. It so happened that because of a secret marriage, she had incurred the Queen's anger and had been banished from Court. Either because she imagined that, with her brother rising in favour, Elizabeth had tacitly forgiven her, or because the less formal atmosphere of a Progress at least offered an opportunity to test the Queen's attitude, Lady Perrott had accepted (if, indeed, she had not engineered) Lady Warwick's invitation.

Here was Raleigh's opportunity. He drew Elizabeth's attention to the disobedience and the Queen immediately ordered Lady Perrott to keep her room. Essex, realizing the implications, flew into a rage and accused the Queen of doing what she had done 'only to please that knave Raleigh, for whose sake I saw she would both grieve me and my love and disgrace me in the eye of the world'.

Elizabeth immediately defended Raleigh 'and it seemed'—so Essex recorded it—'she could not well endure anything to be spoken against him; and taking hold of one word, 'Disdain', she said there was 'no such cause why I should disdain him'.

This only further incensed Essex who, deliberately raising his voice so that Raleigh, on duty the other side of the door as Captain of the Guard, could not avoid hearing him, described as offensively as he could 'what Raleigh had been and what he was'; and asked: 'What comfort can I have to give myself over to a mistress that is in awe of such a man?' and told her: 'I have no joy to be in any place, but am loth to be near about you, when I know my affection so much thrown down and such a wretch as Raleigh highly esteemed of you.' Elizabeth, as angry as Essex, turned from defence to attack and, after some scorching remarks about Essex's sister and his mother (whom, as Leicester's second wife, she in any case detested), refused to continue the conversation, 'but turned her away to my Lady Warwick'. Essex rushed from the room, sent his sister from the house under an escort of his retainers and himself rode off to Margate to take ship for Holland and the wars, saying that a good death was better than a disquiet life. He was, however, overtaken by one of the Queen's couriers before he embarked, brought back and reconciled to Elizabeth. But she would still hear nothing against Raleigh and made every effort to drive Essex into friendship with him—'which rather', as Essex remarked, 'shall drive me to many other extremities'.

Officially Raleigh could not have heard the conversation which Essex had taken care he could not miss, and thus he was prevented from answering it by a challenge to a duel. (Such a challenge he made, on another pretext, the following year, but the Privy Council intervened to stop the fight.) But he made a contemptuous answer in words to the words that had overtopped the rest. On a scrap of paper he wrote:

If Cynthia be a Queen, a princess and supreme,
Keep these among the rest, or say it was a dream.
For those that like, expound, and those that loathe, express

Meanings according as their minds are movéd more or less.
For writing 'what thou art' or showing 'what thou were'
Adds to the one 'Disdain', to th' other but 'Despair'.
Thy mind of neither needs, in both seeing it exceeds.

Until M. C. Bradbrook[1] pointed out that the verse was obviously related to this situation, it was always considered a detached and incomprehensible riddle. Its full meaning is still far from clear, though it appears to be addressed indirectly to the Queen, and, repeating the phrases of Essex's tirade, asserts his own disdain of the new favourite and his own despair at the favour shown him.

Such allusive, riddling verses were one of the Court fashions and Raleigh naturally composed them as well as any other. He had written one, which could be read either across or downwards, beginning:

Your face	*your tongue*	*your wit*
So fair	*so sweet*	*so sharp*
First bent	*then drew*	*so hit*
Mine eye	*mine ear*	*my heart*
Mine eye	*mine ear*	*my heart*
To like	*to learn*	*to love*
Your face	*your tongue*	*your wit*
Doth lead	*doth teach*	*doth move*

and so on for six patterned, intricate verses.

He had made another, which seems to have some reference to those early words he scratched on the window, beginning:

[1] In *The School of Night* (1936)

Fain would I, but I dare not
I dare, but yet I may not.
I may although I care not
For pleasure when I play not.

You laugh, because you like not.
I jest and yet I joy not.
You pierce, although you strike not.
I strike and yet annoy not.

This method of playing with words and 'conceits' was probably more typical of Raleigh, as his contemporaries knew him, than we, at this distance and with very few manuscripts to judge by, can fully realize; for when the young Shakespeare, a few years later, caricatured him in *Love's Labour's Lost* he put in his mouth this exposition of the story of King Cophetua and the Beggar Maid: 'He came, saw and overcame. He came, one; saw, two; overcame, three. Who came? the King. Why did he come? to see. Why did he see? to overcome. To whom came he? to the beggar. Who overcame he? the beggar. The conclusion is victory. On whose side? the King's: the captive is enriched. On whose side? the beggar's. The catastrophe is a nuptial. On whose side? the King's?—no, on both in one or one in both.'

It was, perhaps, a deserved satire. Yet underneath the mere arranger of words, the poet still lay; and it was probably about this time that, seeing his position and all he fought for endangered by his youthful rival, Raleigh reflected on the mutability of life and the certainty of death in the first draft of an unforgettable poem.

ESSEX

Even such is Time, which takes in trust
　Our youth, our joys, and all we have,
And pays us but with age and dust,
　Who in the dark and silent grave,
　　When we have wandered all our ways,
　　Shuts up the story of our days.

CHAPTER SIX

THE ARMADA, AND THE
PORTUGAL VOYAGE

T he year 1588, the year of Spain's Great Armada
against England, put a temporary stop to Court
bickerings. The menace of foreign invasion left
no room for lesser alarums and Raleigh found himself at
last allowed action. War with Spain had been inevitable
since Drake, in 1587, had decimated the Spanish fleet in
harbour and forced Philip II to initiate in earnest the great
'Enterprise of England' which was to clear the sea of English pirates by attacking their base and make possible
Spain's peaceful development of the New World.

Elizabeth took steps to prepare for the expected assault
and in the November of 1587 called a special Council of
War, on which Raleigh served, to discuss them. Raleigh
himself drew up a list of places particularly open to invasion and, after acting as general adviser in the matter of
fortifications—in which capacity he went as far away
from his own territory as Norfolk—rode down to Devon
and Cornwall to raise troops of foot and horse to repel a
possible Spanish landing.

Early in 1588, however, it seemed for a moment that
the alarm was a false one and he took advantage of the
lull (combined with the circumstance that at last, after six

years, Elizabeth found she could bear his absence with equanimity) to visit his estates in Ireland, where he acted as Mayor of Youghal. But the diplomatic skies soon darkened again and he had to hurry back to continue preparations to repulse the Armada.

It appeared at last, that great fleet, off Cornwall on the afternoon of the 20th of July 1588, and that night under cover of darkness sixty little English ships put out from Plymouth to engage it in a week-long running fight up the Channel. Raleigh was not among them; his duties of organization kept him on land. But his own ships played their part in the battle—his *Ark Raleigh* was the flagship of the Admiral, Lord Howard; his *Roebuck* carried powder to the fleet—and, as soon as the Armada had passed Devon and any danger of invasion there was over, he rushed up to London and begged to be allowed to join the fight in the capacity of a volunteer aboard the *Ark Raleigh*. This, however, was not permitted and not until news arrived that the Spaniards were stranded before Gravelines did the Queen send him 'with all speed to order the Admiral to attack the Armada in some way, or to engage it if he could not burn it'.

But it was precisely by not engaging the Armada in the conventional manner—ship grappling ship and fighting the matter out as opposing troops on an artificial island—that the victory was to be won. The Spaniards, with their immense superiority, would have welcomed such a move. And Raleigh, years later, left in his *History of the World*, an account of the English tactics which he noticed that day when at last he boarded the ship he had built.

'There is a good deal of difference', he wrote, 'between fighting loose or at large and grappling. To clap ships together without consideration belongs rather to a madman than to a man of war; for by such an ignorant bravery was Peter Strozzi lost at the Azores when he fought against the Marquess of Santa Cruz. In like sort had Charles Howard, Admiral of England, been lost in the year 1588, if he had not been better advised than a great many malignant fools were that found fault with his demeanour. The Spaniards had an army aboard them, and he had none; they had more ships than he had and of higher building and charging; so that, had he entangled himself with those great and powerful vessels, he had greatly endangered this kingdom of England. For twenty men upon the defences are equal to a hundred that board and enter; whereas then the Spaniards, contrariwise, had a hundred for twenty of ours to defend themselves withal. But our admiral knew his advantage and held it; which had he not done he had not been worthy to have held his head.'

When the Armada had been finally dispersed and was sailing in disorder to the North, Raleigh urged the Queen to let the fleet follow it and complete its destruction, lest the Spaniards should manage to put in to Denmark and, after rest and refitting, return to the attack. Though he was over-ruled in this, in the following year it was decided to send an expedition against Spain. Drake, who had been the real hero of the defeat of the Armada, was to lead it, and this time Raleigh was given royal permission to go with him. It was now Essex who was kept at home.

Essex, however, gave one more proof of his peculiar temperament. He slipped away from Court in disguise, rode 220 miles in thirty-six hours and so outdistanced the couriers sent to stop him, avoided the main fleet, which

THE ARMADA, AND PORTUGAL VOYAGE

was in Plymouth, and took ship at Falmouth in the *Swiftsure*, under the command of his friend Sir Roger Williams. The *Swiftsure* immediately put out to sea, and did not make contact with Drake and Raleigh for five weeks, during which time, at the furious Queen's command, the Channel had been scoured for him, Williams threatened with death and Drake told that he could now bear personally most of the costs of the campaign.

Essex's motive was strictly financial. As he said in a note he left for his grandfather: 'My revenue is no greater than when I sued my livery; my debts at the least two or three and twenty thousand pounds; Her Majesty's goodness hath been so great as I could not ask more of her; no way left to repair myself but mine own adventure. . . . If I should speed well, I will adventure to be rich; if not, I will never live to see the end of my poverty.' In this, he was no different from any other participator in the enterprise, the object of which was, quite openly, loot, though the official excuse given was the restoration to the throne of Portugal of the pretender, Dom Antonio, who had been kicking his heels in England for the last eight years.

The campaign, of no particular interest in itself, concerns this narrative only in so far as it illustrates a new element in the relationship of Raleigh and Essex. It is the first of three occasions when they served together in an official pillaging expedition; and throughout the series the pattern remains the same. Raleigh makes the right decision, Essex the wrong one; yet Raleigh always defers to Essex and, as comrade-in-arms, shows friendship—even an admiration—for him, which is in striking contrast to his usual attitude.

In the Portugal voyage, Drake, seconded by Raleigh,

proposed to force the Tagus and sack Lisbon by sea.
Essex, seconded by Dom Antonio, insisted that they
should march overland. Essex did so, lost six thousand
men by disease, desertion and enemy attack—for the Por-
tuguese showed no desire to be liberated from Spain—
and failed even to make an assault on Lisbon. Raleigh and
Drake, meanwhile, swept the enemy shipping off the
seas, burnt two hundred vessels in the Tagus estuary and
captured several prizes.

Yet—and here enters another factor which recurs
throughout their relationship—the legend arose that whatever Essex did was well done. To the end of his life,
Essex retained the enthusiasm, almost the worship, of
those who knew him only as a public figure. Almost to
the end, Raleigh, for whom those who really knew him
would risk death, monotonously aroused the fury of the
mob. Though this was to be expected, since contemporary
popular judgments are always wrong—'the crowd', as the
philosopher has said, '*is* untruth'—there can seldom have
been a case in history of a more obvious double error and
one which, moreover, affected subsequent judgments.
But, even at the time, Raleigh aided the growth of the
Essex legend by describing his foolish and abortive advance on Lisbon as a fine exploit. It was the tribute of
courage to courage.

Those who knew the truth, however, were more dis-
criminating. On the return of the expedition, the Queen
gave Raleigh a gold chain, which was correctly interpreted as an intended snub to Essex. And in Spain, it was
Raleigh's name that was henceforth coupled with
Drake's as that of a dreaded English leader.

CHAPTER SEVEN

'THE SHEPHERD OF THE OCEAN'

The atmosphere of Court intrigue and rivalries soon reasserted itself. Shortly after the defeat of the Armada, Leicester had died, and with his passing, something irreplaceable went out of the Queen's life. No one did, because no one could, take the place with her of this girlhood's love whom only diplomatic necessity had prevented her from marrying. But with Leicester gone, the favouriteship might well be thought to carry with it an increased power and therefore was the more important to whichever of them—Raleigh or Essex—managed to hold it.

The first round went to Essex. He was pardoned for his Portugal exploit and Raleigh went back to Ireland. The Court gossips reported it in terms that might have been expected and may have been true: 'My Lord of Essex hath chased Mr. Raleigh from the Court and confined him to Ireland.' Raleigh, however, gave a different explanation to one of his cousins: 'For my retreat from Court, it was upon good cause; to take order for my prize', and certainly he spent his time on his Irish estates—the last six months of 1589—in ordering his property. He rebuilt Lismore Castle, made experiments in mining, drained bogs, planted trees, studied crops and plants—and introduced the potato.

'THE SHEPHERD OF THE OCEAN'

None of these things, however, are the reason that this short, peaceful stay in Ireland is remembered. Its importance is in its contribution to the literature of England. Raleigh's neighbour, living at Kilcolman Castle, was the greatest of contemporary poets, Edmund Spenser. He and Raleigh were the same age and may have met casually during Raleigh's campaigning days in Ireland, when Spenser was Lord Grey's secretary. Now Spenser, after some time in London, when he had both established his poetic reputation by *The Shepherd's Calendar* and incurred Burleigh's anger by a satire on the Anjou wooing in which he had represented Burleigh as a fox, had returned disconsolately to comparative poverty in Ireland and was engaged on a new poem called *The Faerie Queen*.

When Raleigh rode over to visit him at Kilcolman, he showed him as much as he had completed of the poem. Raleigh's enthusiasm was intense. Here, as he at once recognized, was the epic which should immortalize the Elizabethan age, as Virgil had immortalized the Augustan. Spenser must return with him to England, where he would introduce him to Elizabeth to offer her the work in person.

On the face of it, the relationship of Raleigh to Spenser was that of Court patron to poor poet; but, because Raleigh, too, was a 'maker' the meeting developed into an equal friendship in the free republic of art. They paid each other sugared compliments in verse. For Raleigh, too, was writing. Catching fire, it may be, from Spenser, it was now that Raleigh the poet threw off the mask of Court versifier and began his own long poem, *The Ocean's Love to Cynthia*, of which the first ten books—those that he wrote now in Ireland—are lost and only the eleventh

and part of the twelfth have been preserved to give us a
measure of their quality.

Spenser, in *Colin Clout's Come Home Again*, refers to
this poem:

> *His song was all a lamentable lay*
> *Of great unkindness and of usage hard,*
> *Of Cynthia, the Lady of the Sea,*
> *Which from her presence faultless him debarred,*
> *And ever and anon, with singults[1] rife,*
> *He criéd out to make his undersong,*
> *'Ah, my love's Queen and goddess of my life.'*
> *Who shall me pity when thou dost me wrong?*

—a picture which incidentally suggests that the gossips
were not altogether wrong in their suggestions as to why
he was in Ireland.

In the same poem, writing in the convention of shep-
herds piping in Arcady, Spenser records Raleigh's visit to
him, his enthusiasm on reading *The Faerie Queen*, his
writing of *Cynthia* and their reading of their works in
progress to each other:

> *I sat (as was my trade)*
> *Under the foot of Mole, that mountain hoar,*
> *Keeping my sheep amongst the cooling shade*
> *Of the green alders by the Mulla's shore.*
> *There a strange shepherd chanced to find me out,*
> *Whether alluréd with my pipe's delight,*
> *Whose pleasing sound yshrilléd far about,*
> *Or thither led by chance, I know not right,*
> *Who, when I asked from what place he came,*

[1] Sighs

52

'THE SHEPHERD OF THE OCEAN'

And how he hight, himself he did yclepe
The Shepheard of the Oceān by name
And said he came far from the main-sea deep.
He sitting me beside in that same shade,
Provokéd me to play some pleasant fit;
And when he heard the music that I made
He found himself full greatly pleased at it.
Yet, emuling my pipe, he took in hond
My pipe (before that emuléd of many)
And played thereon (for well that skill he conn'd),
Himself as skilful in that art as any.
He piped, I sung; and when he sung, I piped;
By change of turns, each making other merry,
Neither envying other nor envyd—
So piped we, until we both were weary.

As once, at the outset of his career, Raleigh had written
a prefatory verse for Gascoigne's poem, hoping by it to
bring himself into notice, so now from his worldly
eminence, he gave help by prefacing *The Faerie Queen*
with a sonnet:

Methought I saw the grave where Laura lay,
Wherein that Temple with the vestal flame
Was wont to burn; and, passing by that way,
To see that buried dust of living fame,
Whose tomb fair Love and fairer Virtue kept,
All suddenly I saw the Faery Queen
At whose approach the soul of Petrarch wept.
And from henceforth those Graces were not seen
(For they this Queen attended) in whose stead
Oblivion laid him down on Laura's hearse.
Hereat the hardest stones were seen to bleed,

53

And groans of buried ghosts the heavens did pierce,
  Where Homer's spright did tremble all for grief,
  And curse the access of that celestial thief.

Spenser replied to Raleigh's hyperbolic description of him as a 'celestial thief' whose entrance into the highest heaven of poetry made even Homer afraid by one of the most charming names that even the Elizabethans invented, in a sonnet protesting, courteously, that *The Faerie Queen* was inferior to *Cynthia*:

To thee, that art the Summer's Nightingale,
Thy sovereign Goddess's most dear delight,
Why do I send this rustic Madrigal,
  That may thy tuneful ear unseason quite,
  Thou only fit this Argument to write,
In whose high thoughts Pleasure hath built her bower
  And dainty Love learnt sweetly to indite!
My rhymes I know unsavoury and sour
To taste the streams that like a golden shower
  Flow from thy fruitful head, of thy Love's praise
(Fitter, perhaps, to thunder martial stower,
  Whenso thee list thy lofty Muse to raise).
    Yet, till that thou thy Poem wilt make known,
    Let thy fair Cynthia's praises be thus rudely shown.

Since the poem has not, even yet, been made known, we are not in a position to judge their respective merits, though the fragment of *The Ocean's Love to Cynthia* we possess does not suggest even an equality with *The Faerie Queen*; yet in it there are passages and images which haunt the memory as certainly as those of Spenser:

Like to a falling stream which passing slow
Is wont to nourish sleep and quietness

'THE SHEPHERD OF THE OCEAN'

or

To seek new worlds, for gold, for praise, for glory,
To try desire, to try love severed far.
When I was gone she sent her memory,
More strong than were ten thousand ships of war.

or

The weal, the woe, the passages of old
And worlds of thought described by one last sighing.

When Raleigh brought Spenser back to Court, it was two poets who came home.

Elizabeth welcomed and forgave Raleigh, shared his enthusiasm for *The Faerie Queen* (of which the first three books were published in 1590) and granted the author a pension of £50. Burleigh, quite apart from his unforgiving dislike of Spenser, was scandalized. 'All this for a song!' he remonstrated. 'It is beyond reason.' 'Then give him what is within reason,' said the Queen. Burleigh decided that this could be interpreted as nothing and made no payment. After waiting for some time, Spenser wrote to Elizabeth:

I was promised on a time
To have reason for my rhyme;
Since that time, until this season,
I have had nor rhyme nor reason.

Though the epigram is his, it is difficult not to suspect a consultation with Raleigh. Elizabeth called Burleigh to account and the unhandsome £50 was paid.

To Raleigh, pleading for Spenser, Elizabeth said: 'When will you cease to be a beggar?'

'When your gracious Majesty', answered Raleigh, 'ceases to be a benefactor.'

CHAPTER EIGHT

PRIVATEERING EXPEDITIONS

Raleigh was back in favour and remained so for two years. At the beginning of 1590, when he returned from Ireland, his rival made the major mistake of getting married. Such an action, as Essex should have known better than anyone, was certain to provoke the Queen to the most violent anger; for when Elizabeth had discovered his own mother's marriage to Leicester, some years earlier, her rage had passed all bounds of decency and she had immediately imprisoned Leicester and banished his wife from Court. When Essex, by marrying the widow of Sir Philip Sidney, repeated the pattern of his step-father's offence—even to the detail of keeping it secret from the Queen as long as he could—the Royal storm again broke; and though, on condition that his wife never appeared at Court, Elizabeth eventually forgave him, she calmly allowed him to go with a small force of volunteers to aid the Huguenots in the continuing civil war in France, from which he did not return (after a display of his usual disastrous incompetence) till the January of 1592. This time it was Raleigh who, once more, was kept at home.

He was occupied, apart from the usual routine of the Court in which he played his accustomed part more splendid and more saturnine than ever, in organizing privateering expeditions as part of the continuing war with Spain. It had been decided that the simplest way to embarrass Spain and enrich England, without risking the consequences of a full-scale naval war, was to waylay Spanish treasure ships on their way home from America. So successful had the policy proved that the King Philip had forbidden his West Indian fleet to sail in 1590, with the result that Spain went practically bankrupt. Elizabeth and her advisers correctly assumed that he would not repeat the policy of abstention in 1591 and an English expedition was prepared to sail for the Azores to intercept and plunder the Spanish silver fleet. Lord Thomas Howard was put in command and Raleigh was to sail with it as Vice-Admiral in his ship, the *Revenge*. Or so, at least, the Queen led him to believe till the last moment, when she refused to let him go and made him send his cousin, Sir Richard Grenville, in his place.

The upshot of this expedition every schoolboy knows, for the last fight of the *Revenge* and the death of Sir Richard Grenville have pride of place in the Elizabethan epic. But not every schoolboy realizes that it was Raleigh who gave them that place and that it is his first published work, the *Report of the Truth of the Fight about the Azores*, written immediately to defend his cousin's memory, that is the basis of Tennyson's famous ballad.

What the planners of the expedition had not allowed for was a change in Spanish policy. This time nothing was left to chance and the silver fleet was accompanied by fifty-three warships against which the *Revenge*, covering the flight of the rest of the English ships, fought its last, stupendous action. Grenville could, had he wished, have escaped, even at the last moment, by flight, but, as Raleigh wrote: 'Sir Richard utterly refused to turn from the enemy, alleging that he would rather choose to die than to dishonour himself, his country and Her Majesty's ship, persuading the company that he would pass through the two Squadrons in despite of them; and enforce those of Seville to give way to him.'

So started the fight 'of the one and the fifty-three', in which for fifteen hours, the hundred and twenty men of the *Revenge* fought off the Spanish ships and killed a thousand of the enemy, until, with ammunition gone and the *Revenge* reduced to a helpless, drifting raft, she was boarded by the men of the giant *Saint Philip* and Grenville and the survivors taken aboard as prisoners. Grenville lived for three days, impressing his captors (who regarded him as a child of the Devil) by crushing wineglasses between his fingers until the blood ran and swallowing the splinters. Then, at the end, he made his immortal farewell, as Raleigh records it from the report of a witness: 'Here die I, Richard Grenville, with a joyful and quiet mind, for that I have ended my life as a true soldier ought to do that hath fought for his country, Queen, religion and honour, whereby my soul departeth most joyfully out of this body and shall always leave behind it an everlasting fame as a valiant and true soldier that hath done his duty as he was bound to do.'

Though the attack on the silver fleet failed, Raleigh's minor expeditions that year were not altogether unsuccessful and one of his captains brought home merchandise to the value of £31,150, of which he took his tenth, £3,015; the sailors divided £10,383; the Queen took £1,600; £1,200 was estimated as the cost of bringing home the goods and the rest—£14,952—was divided among the twelve shipowners and victuallers who had gone into partnership with him.

The Queen now encouraged him to fit out a new expedition for 1592 to capture that year's silver fleet and to sack Panama. She herself contributed money to it, besides lending him some of her own ships—including his *Ark Raleigh*, now the *Ark Royal*, which she had bought from him—and compelling several London merchants to invest large sums in the enterprise. She also promised not only to let him accompany the expedition but to lead it, as Admiral; and through the winter Raleigh, happy that his dearest wish was at last on the verge of fulfilment, travelled backwards and forwards between London and Plymouth, making detailed preparations for the voyage. In the January of 1592 she gave him, in addition, her greatest gift—Sherborne Castle—the lovely Dorset estate which was to be his home till the end of his life. And as this gesture coincided with the return of Essex from France, it might be interpreted as setting the seal on Raleigh's position as undisputed favourite.

He sailed, an Admiral at last, on the 6th May 1592, though he knew it was for a few days only. For once more Elizabeth changed her mind and would not let him go. As early as March she had told him that she wished him merely to start the expedition and then to relinquish his position to Frobisher (who, as an unpopular leader, would not in the preparatory stage have commanded the confidence of either sailors or investors). Though Frobisher overtook him on May 7th, Raleigh still held on as far as Cape Finisterre, spending the time in planning the operations, and, determined not to repeat the error of the previous year, ordering the fleet to split in two, so that one part of it could divert the Spaniards on their own coast while the other waylaid the silver fleet.

Only when he had laid the foundation of success did he return, reluctantly and tardily, to London. He was immediately sent to the Tower.

CHAPTER NINE

ELIZABETH THROCKMORTON

The punishment was not unexpected. A month or two before he had sailed—the exact date is uncertain—he had, despite the warning examples of Leicester and Essex, committed the unforgiveable crime. He had secretly married Elizabeth Throckmorton, one of the Queen's Maids of Honour. Court and country buzzed with the news, rejoicing in the prospect of Raleigh's impending and final fall. A letter of the time, written while he was still at sea, gives a clear enough picture of it.

'S.W.R., as it seemeth,' says the writer, 'hath been too inward with one of Her Majesty's Maids; I fear to say who, but if you should guess at E.T. you may not be far wrong. The matter hath only now been apparent to all eyes, and the lady hath been sent away, but nobody believes it can end there. S.W.R. hath escaped from London for a time; he will be speedily sent for and brought back, where what awaiteth him nobody knoweth, save by conjecture. All think the Tower will be his dwelling, like hermit poor in pensive place, where he may spend his endless days in doubt. It is affirmed that they are married; but the Queen is most fiercely incensed, and, as the bruit goes, threateneth the most bitter punishment to both the offenders. S.W.R. will lose, it is thought, all his places and preferments at Court, with the Queen's favour; such

will be the end of his speedy rising, and now he must fall
as low as he was high, at the which many will rejoice. I
can write no more at this time, and do not care to send
this, only you will hear it from others. All is alarm and
confusion at this discovery of the discoverer, and not indeed of a new continent, but of a new incontinent.'

The marriage was a love-match and never, before it or
after, was Raleigh's name in that age and court of scandal, connected with that of any other woman. Years
later, under the shadow of death, he wrote to her: 'I chose
you and I loved you in my happiest times,' and that is
perhaps the best epitome of it. At the height of his fortune, he chose to lose it for love.

Elizabeth Throckmorton was not particularly beautiful. She never pretended to understand him in his genius
and his dreams, but she gave him quiet care, unwavering
loyalty and a courage that matched his own. The 'happy
times' were not to come again for them and their twenty-
six years of married life were to be lived in the shadows of
uncertainty and disgrace, separation and imprisonment.
Yet her fortitude and gay trust in him never wavered;
she fought the world for him while he was alive and,
when he was dead, continued to fight for his memory
through her long widowhood. With the scaffold loom-
ing, he was to write to her: 'My love I send you that you
may keep it when I am dead, and my counsel, that you
may remember it when I am no more. I would not with
my last will present you with sorrows, dear Bess. Let
them go to the grave with me and be buried in the dust.
And, seeing it is not the will of God that ever I shall see
you in this life, bear my destruction gently and with a
heart like yourself.' And now, as they spent their honey-

moon in prison, a new note came into his poetry. Though the poem was ostensibly concerned with Elizabeth Tudor, there can be little doubt that it was Elizabeth Raleigh who inspired:

> But Love is a durable fire
> In the mind ever burning;
> Never sick, never old, never dead,
> From itself never turning.

The emotions which existed at this time between Raleigh and the Queen can be conjectured only. It is probable that, although he knew that he risked disgrace, he underestimated the strength of her fury. He may well have imagined that his marriage would affect her less than had those of Leicester and Essex, both of which had eventually been forgiven. In the event, it seems to have hurt her more. She had never had any illusions about Leicester's philanderings and it was, in a sense, proper that Essex, as a young nobleman, should give his house an heir. But for Raleigh, apparently a confirmed bachelor at the age of forty, dependent on her for all he had, to make a very ordinary marriage, suggested only one explanation, the explanation which, in fact, was true—that he had loved and chosen his wife in his happiest days. In face of this, all his protestations were of no value. She accepted his wild outbursts in the spirit in which it may be suspected he made them—as the gallantries of a master-courtier, still playing the expected game but with the heart gone out of it.

For, of course, Raleigh made protestations. In prison, his one object was to get out and only the Queen could release him. Nor was she likely to do so unless such an action could be appropriately adjusted to the pattern of their relationship. He repeated the extravagances of their meeting, ten years earlier. On hearing that Elizabeth would be passing the Tower in her barge on the way to Richmond, he begged his keeper (who was also one of his cousins) that he might be rowed out at least near enough to gaze on the Goddess. When refused, he went temporarily mad and attempted to kill himself, but was prevented by another cousin, Sir Arthur Gorges, whose hand was slashed by his dagger in consequence. Or so his keeper reported to the Queen, adding: 'Sir Walter Raleigh will shortly grow to be "Orlando Furioso" if the bright Angelica persevere against him a little longer.'

On another occasion, being informed that the Queen was setting out on her summer Progress, he wrote in a letter that he knew she would read: 'My heart was never broken till this day that I hear the Queen goes so far off, whom I have followed so many years with so great love and desire in so many journeys, and am now left behind her in a dark prison all alone. While she was yet near at hand that I might hear of her once in two or three days, my sorrows were less, but even now my heart is cast into the depth of all misery. I that was wont to behold her riding like Alexander, hunting like Diana, walking like Venus, the gentle wind blowing her fair hair about her pure cheeks like a nymph! sometimes sitting in the shade like a goddess! sometimes singing like an angel! sometimes playing like Orpheus! Behold the sorrow of this world! One amiss hath bereaved me of all. . . . She is gone in whom I trusted, and of me hath not one thought of mercy, nor any respect of that that was. Do with me therefore what you list. I am more weary of life than they are desirous that I should perish, which, if it had been for her as it is by her, I had been too happily born.'

More importantly, Raleigh in prison returned to writing *Cynthia* and completed the portion of it that we now possess. His 'Lady of the Sea' was more unkind than she had been even in his Irish exile; but he had with him that other lady, whose love gave to his poetry a note of genuine passion. With her, when at last in the autumn of 1592 they were released, he retired to Sherborne which together they made into a perfect home. There, building and rebuilding, planting cedars from Virginia and shrubs from the tropics, so that even to-day, as one of his biographers has said, Raleigh's 'very spirit hovers there amongst the bricks he laid', they lived in exile from Court; and there, in 1594, their son, Walter, was born.

CHAPTER TEN

THE GREAT CARRACK

Raleigh's release was not due to any relenting on the part of the Queen. He was given his liberty for a severely practical reason. His expedition had captured a treasure ship.

The plan of campaign he had outlined before he left the command to Frobisher had been followed. While the Admiral had watched the Spanish coast, the Vice-Admiral had sailed for the Azores and there had captured an East Indian carrack, the *Madre de Dios*, which had proved to be the richest single prize ever taken. She was 'a floating castle with nearly 800 inhabitants'. Her cargo consisted of pepper and cloves and cinnamon, cochineal, mace, nutmegs and musk. The pepper alone was worth £102,000. But there were also precious stones, pearls, amber and ebony; satins, tapestries and silks. It took ten English ships eventually to carry the fabulous cargo from Dartmouth to London—and by that time a portion of it had disappeared. For when the Great Carrack was towed into Dartmouth, there was an outburst of looting on a county-wide scale. The West Country went mad 'for jewels, pearls and amber'. One sailor alone was found in possession of 'a chain of orient pearls, two chains of gold, four great pearls of the bigness of a fair pea, four forks of crystal and four spoons of crystal set with gold and stones, and two cords of musk'. Other plunderers had bags of rubies and diamonds. Every man on the road going east 'did smeall of prizes'—musk and ambergris—and, rushing to meet them were over two thousand merchants and goldsmiths, in wild competition to buy what they could as cheaply as they could from the simple sailors. In one such bargain, 1,800 diamonds and 300 rubies went for £130!

Order had somehow to be restored or the treasure, enormous as it was, would little by little, melt away. To attempt to enforce the law was quite useless. Putting the sailors on their oath was 'lost labour and offence to God', and they were more than indifferent to the protestations of their commanders. The Queen sent Burleigh's son, Robert Cecil, armed with all the authority of London, but he was as powerless as anyone else. It was clear that Raleigh—whose expedition, after all, it was—was the only man who could cope with the situation, especially as the sailors' lawlessness was increased by their indignation at hearing he was in prison. So, discreetly accompanied by his keeper, Raleigh went.

Cecil, in a letter, described his reception at Dartmouth: 'I assure you sir, his poor servants, to the number of 140 godly men, and all the mariners came to him with such shouts of joy as I never heard a man more troubled to quiet them in my life. But his heart is broken for he is very extreme pensive, longer than he is busied, in which he can toil terribly. The meeting between him and Sir John Gilbert[1] was with tears on Sir John's part. Whensoever he is saluted with congratulations for liberty, he doth answer: "No, I am still the Queen of England's poor

---

[1] His half-brother, younger brother of Sir Humphrey.

captive." I wished him to conceal it, because here it doth diminish his credit, which I do vow to you before God is greater among the mariners than I thought for.'

Meanwhile Raleigh himself wrote to Burleigh a letter intended to leave no doubt that he was taking this opportunity of striking a bargain. He asked 'in particular how Her Majesty might be profited by the Carrack, according to the offer I made. My promise was not to buy my bondage but my liberty, and, I hope, of Her Majesty's favour. . . . Fourscore thousand pounds is more than ever a man presented Her Majesty as yet. If God have sent it for my ransom, I hope Her Majesty will accept it.'

But if he could bargain, so could she. In the end, she got half of the entire booty and he got nothing except his freedom.

CHAPTER ELEVEN

'THE SCHOOL OF NIGHT'

Raleigh was not allowed to appear at Court for five years and his duties as Captain of the Guard had to be performed by deputy; but he still, of course, was constantly in London and, as Member of Parliament, his voice, though silenced at Court, was heard in the Commons. In the April of 1593, he protested against a bill proposing to put all Brownists (or, as they would now be called, Congregationalists) to death. 'The law is hard', he said, 'that taketh life, or sendeth into banishment, where men's intentions shall be judged by a jury, or they shall be judges what another man meant.'

Though he had no particular sympathy with the beliefs of the Brownists, this plea against giving twelve ordinary men the right to judge and penalize the theological speculations of others came from his heart and he of all men had, during 1593 and 1594, most need of the safeguard for which he pleaded. At that very moment the Privy Council were preparing to arrest his friend, Christopher Marlowe, the greatest dramatist of the day, on charges of blasphemy and atheism; and when, the following month, Marlowe was killed in a tavern brawl before the case opened, Raleigh was suspected of having a hand in his death to prevent any revelations he might have made under torture. As it was, after Marlowe's death a

Commission on Atheism was set up at Cerne Abbas, not far from Sherborne, to investigate the attitude of Marlowe, Raleigh and others to conventional beliefs and so to bring into the open that society about which the wildest rumours were playing, Raleigh's 'School of Night'.

The 'School of Night' might be described in modern terms as a cross between a club and a learned society. Its members were friends bound together by their intellectual interests. It had no definite political significance, though naturally, with Raleigh as its patron, it came into conflict with the Essex House set, to which the young William Shakespeare had attached himself as a hack playwright. '*Love's Labour's Lost*' was, among other things, Shakespeare's account of the School of Night', though the parody bore little relation to the reality. The outstanding personality in the School, whose genius bound the rest together, was the astronomer and mathematician, Thomas Harriot, whom we have already noticed. (There is reason to suppose that he is the original of Shakespeare's Holofernes.) Sharing his interests were two eccentric noblemen, the thirty-year-old Earl of Northumberland, whose scientific experiments earned him the nickname of 'the Wizard Earl', and the thirty-four-year-old Earl of Derby, poet, alchemist and suspected witch, who died suddenly under circumstances which suggested poison, in 1594. On the literary side, Marlowe was the dramatist of the School (Raleigh served as model for certain aspects of his Dr. Faustus) and George Chapman, a strange, retiring figure, more interested in mysticism than mathematics, became its chief poet and dramatist after Marlowe's murder. Spenser, during his time in London, must be accounted a member of the group, which included also several lesser men whose names need not be mentioned here. The School was dedicated to adventures as daring as any of Raleigh's other enterprises—but these were adventures of the mind and spirit. It questioned everything, from the structure of the Bible to the structure of the Universe, and it brought together in its studies various trends of thought which made that age a ferment of excitement to which there has been no real parallel since, though modern analogies may help an appreciation of it. The astronomical discoveries of Harriot, combined with the geographical explorations of Raleigh, shattered the old comfortable and comprehensible view of the world. The study of science and the unhindered examination of the Bible led them to speculate as to whether there might have been 'men before Adam' and to notice certain contradictions in the Old Testament narrative—'contrarieties of Scripture' as Marlowe called them. And the new political philosophy of Machiavelli, with its ruthless analysis of the realities of power, clarified the motives of men governing. The result was something like the first impact on conventional concepts of Darwin, Einstein, the 'Higher Criticism' and Marx rolled into one and made additionally sinister by the suspicion of witchcraft.

Harriot became in popular estimation 'that devil' and with him, in necromancy, were classed Northumberland and Derby; Marlowe was the blasphemous atheist, whose violent death was a judgment from Heaven; Raleigh was as well as an atheist indistinguishable from that

> *Damnable fiend of Hell,*
> *Mischievous Machiavel.*

The figure of Machiavelli haunted Elizabethan England

71

—there are about four hundred references to him in the literature of the period—and Elizabethan drama has been defined as 'the terror-stricken meeting of the England of Elizabeth with the Italy of the late Renaissance'. On the stage, the master-Machiavel was to be Shakespeare's Iago; in popular estimation in real life it was Sir Walter Raleigh.

In a limited sense, the identification was not altogether unjust. Raleigh had seen, no less than Machiavelli, the reality beneath the pretence of statecraft; he knew the idealistic phrases used to cover the lowest of motives and he was bitterly contemptuous both of the hypocrites who used them and the fools who were duped by them.

'Those that have been best able to imitate the fox', Machiavelli had written, 'have succeeded best. But it is necessary to be able to disguise this character well, and be a great feigner and dissembler; and men are so simple and so ready to obey present necessities, that one who deceives will always find those who allow themselves to be deceived. . . . It is well to seem pious, faithful, humane, religious, sincere and also to be so; but you must have the mind so watchful that when it is needful to be otherwise you may be able to change to the opposite qualities. . . . A prince must take great care that nothing goes out of his mouth which is not full of the above-named five qualities, and, to see and hear him, he should seem to be all faith, all integrity, all humanity and all religion. And nothing is more necessary than to seem to have this last quality, for men in general judge more by the eyes than by the hands, for everyone can see but very few have to feel. Everybody sees what you appear to be, few feel what you are, and those few will not dare to oppose themselves to the many.'

But although, from the time when his disgrace made it possible for his enemies to illuminate the 'School of Night', Raleigh was known as the Fox, there is another sense in which the epithet was the most unsuitable that could be devised. For the whole point about the Machiavellian is that he conceals his real opinions and courts the favour of the mob he secretly despises. Iago is 'honest Iago', trusted and popular. Raleigh, on the other hand, behaved in precisely the opposite fashion. He made no secret of anything and concealed not even his own honesty. In his great poem, *The Lie*, he propounded Machiavelli's analysis with most un-Machiavellian candour. He imagines himself at the point of death, sending his soul to give his last message to the world:

> *Say to the Court, it glows*
> *And shines like rotten wood;*
> *Say to the Church it shows*
> *What's good and doth no good.*
> *If Church and Court reply,*
> *Then give them both the lie.*

> *Tell potentates they live*
> *Acting by others' action;*
> *Not loved unless they give,*
> *Not strong but by a faction,*
> *If potentates reply,*
> *Give potentates the lie.*

> *Tell men of high condition,*
> *That manage the Estate,*
> *Their purpose is ambition,*

Their practice only hate;
And if they once reply,
Then give them all the lie. . . .

Nor, in private conversation with his Dorsetshire neighbours, did he refrain from theological controversy. At one dinner party he asked, as an innocent inquirer after truth, what the soul was. The Rev. Ralph Ironside quoted the stock definition from Aristotle. Raleigh (who, as his writings show, knew the definition perfectly well and had considered its implications deeply) rejected Aristotle as being 'obscure and intricate'. Ironside then explained simply that the soul was 'a spiritual and immortal substance breathed into man by God'.

'Yes,' said Raleigh, 'but what *is* that spiritual and immortal substance?'

'The soul,' said Ironside.

Raleigh pointed out politely that this was arguing in a circle, to be told by the irritated cleric that all arguments about first principles had to proceed in circles. After allowing it to proceed in that manner for a few more moves and pointing out that mathematical first principles at least could be demonstrated, Sir Walter asked him to say grace —'for that', quoth he, 'is better than this disputation'.

Raleigh and the School were, in fact, making attempts to answer theological and philosophical questions at a level at which the conventional did not even understand that there were questions to be asked. Popular legend saw them merely as an association of rather vulgar atheists, who spelt God backwards and dried tobacco on the leaves of a Bible. Yet it was the dreaded Harriot, suffering from cancer of the lips, who wrote: 'I believe in God Almighty;

I believe that medicine was ordained by Him; I trust the physician as His minister. My faith is sure, my hope is firm. I wait however with patience for everything in its own time according to His Providence.' It was the atheist Marlowe who so understood the nature of the Beatific Vision that he could proclaim: 'All places shall be Hell that is not Heaven.' It was Raleigh who had found it impossible to argue with the foolish parson, who wrote: 'As the fire mounteth of itself upward and is carried round with the heavens, so the soul of man is led upward somewhat by the senses, and doth many things in and out of the body without them; which shows it must have other beginning than this. Is it not a manifest argument that it cometh from God, seeing in all things it resteth not till it come to God? The mind, in searching causes, is never quiet till it come to God, and the will is never satisfied with any good till it come to the immortal goodness.'

Not unnaturally the Commission on Atheism at Cerne Abbas came to nothing and was abandoned; but the other attack on the School in *Love's Labour's Lost* was more successful and lasting. Shakespeare, as the employee of the Essex faction, was at pains to make his picture of Raleigh as wounding as he could. He starts with the supreme insult of representing him as a Spaniard, Don Armado, but he leaves no doubt in the minds of any of the audience who is intended by the knight who spends his time writing poetry, who addresses his servant with a West Country 'Chirrah', who is noted for the magnificence of his dress and for his tales of travel ('I protest I love to hear him lie'), who is short of money and whose 'humour is lofty, his discourse peremptory, his tongue filed, his eye ambitious, his gait majestical, and his general behaviour vain, ridiculous and thrasonical'. To underline the identity, if that were necessary, he introduces the rhyme:

> *The Fox, the Ape and the Humble Bee*
> *Were still at odds, being but three . . .*
> *Until the Goose came out of door*
> *Staying the odds by adding four*

—the Goose being Elizabeth Throckmorton and the other three animals representing aspects of Raleigh, the Fox his Machiavellianism; the Ape his flattery; the Humble Bee his buzzing about the Court. And finally in one couplet he epitomizes Raleigh's dark complexion, his atheism, his recent imprisonment and his School:

> *O paradox! Black is the badge of Hell,*
> *The hue of dungeons and the School of Night.*

Love's Labour's Lost was not the last word, though it has outlasted the others. The School replied with *Willobie, His Avisa*, and throughout 1594 the literary warfare continued. That episode, however, belongs to a study of Elizabethan literature rather than the story of Sir Walter Raleigh.

CHAPTER TWELVE

EL DORADO

A mong other things, the School of Night was suspected of alchemical research for the philosopher's stone which could turn all things to gold. The suspicion was probably correct, at least as far as Northumberland and Derby were concerned, for the quest for knowledge was also a quest for power. In that age, astronomy was but an intermediate step to astrology, as chemistry was to alchemy. It was only the rationalism of a later century that was to reverse the order and so lose understanding of the process. Raleigh's mind, too, was certainly set on gold, but gold to be obtained in a more conventional manner.

One of the travellers' tales which haunted the imagination of Englishmen and Spaniard alike was that of Manoa, the Golden City, standing on the shores of an inland lake in the heart of South America. Here the descendants of the last of the Incas still reigned in splendour, safe from the invaders who had destroyed and annexed their great kingdom. A Spanish officer, condemned to death for negligence, had been marooned on the Orinoco, where the natives had discovered him and taken him as a curiosity to this El Dorado. Here, in this city so vast that the journey from the outer gate to the Inca's palace was a whole day's journey, he had seen the Children of the Sun, their bodies powdered with gold, feasting together. On his report, the Spaniards made expedition after expedition to find the fabled city and some imagined that they had in fact seen it from far off; and although El Dorado came to signify only the myth at the end of the rainbow, it is not certain that they were mistaken. Sir Clements Markham in the nineteenth century could write of 'the probability that the Incas actually did succeed in prolonging their civilization, apart from Spanish contamination, in the vast plains to the eastward of the Andes, for one or two centuries after the time of Pizarro. The same story was told to me when I was on the shores of the Purus in 1853, and my informant pointed to the forests which stretched away to the horizon, at the same time describing a lake, on the banks of which Ynti (the Peruvian deity) still found adorers. It is a pleasant reflection that this story may possibly be true.'

Raleigh, at any rate, believed it true. He examined travellers who had returned across the Atlantic; he studied maps, he sent out one of his trusted lieutenants, Captain Jacob Whiddon, a veteran of his privateering expeditions, to reconnoitre on the Orinoco; and he found a disciple and fellow-enthusiast in Laurence Keymis, the thirty-year-old Notary and Bursar of Balliol. Lady Raleigh became apprehensive about the enthusiasm. She realized that unless her husband was recalled to Court or given some administrative employment Sherborne would give place to El Dorado. She wrote to Cecil asking him to use his influence to 'rather draw Sir Walter towards the east than help him forward toward the sunset, if any respect to me or love to him be not forgotten'. But the Queen remained unforgiving. Raleigh, having discovered by intercepted letters that the Spanish governor of Trinidad was about to send out an expedition to find the Golden City, asked her for a patent to enable him to forestall the Spaniards. She granted it but addressed it to 'our servant Sir Walter Raleigh', with the usual 'trusty and well-beloved' pointedly omitted. Because of the continuing war with Spain, the patent was, however, drawn up with greater latitude than usual. Raleigh was still 'to discover and subdue heathen lands not in possession of any Christian prince or inhabited by any Christian people', but he was also permitted 'to offend and enfeeble the King of Spain' and 'to resist and expel' anyone who settled within 200 leagues of his new colony.

Raleigh's motives in undertaking this new expedition were mixed. Predominating was the desire for personal wealth and his consequent rehabilitation with the Queen. If the Great Carrack had bought his pardon, what would not be accomplished by the present of a fabulous empire of gold, by comparison with which the Carrack's treasures were a mere speck of dust? But there was also the desire to go adventuring at last, to be able to see with his own eyes, after so many prohibitions and frustrations, the lands which he knew so well by report and which by reputation were associated with his name. His admirers also insist that, in attempting to claim Guiana for England, he was initiating a new policy; that he had realized that sporadic piracy and plunder were not enough and that if England was effectually to rival Spain she, too, must find a great reservoir of wealth on which she could permanently depend. It may be so, though it may be suspected that, for Raleigh, the simpler reasons sufficed.

Although the expedition was ready to sail in the autumn

of 1594, it did not actually set out—because of the usual series of obstacles and ill luck—till the February of 1595. On March 22nd, Raleigh, accompanied by Kemys, landed in Trinidad. He went ashore at Curapan, the same spot where, nearly a century before, Columbus, too, first stood upon the soil of the New World.

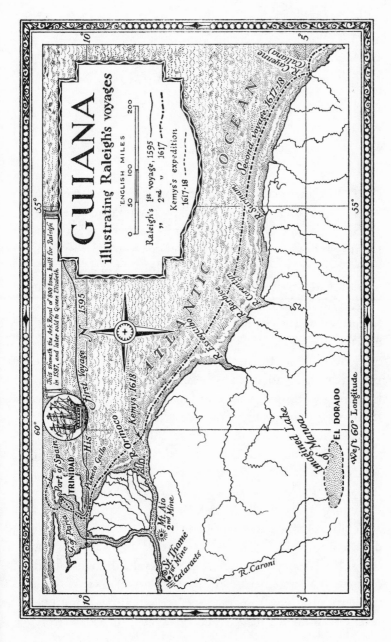

GUIANA
illustrating Raleigh's voyages

ENGLISH MILES
0   50   100   200

Raleigh's 1st voyage, 1595
"   2nd "   1617
Kemys's expedition
1617-18

This sheweth the Ark Royal of 800 tons, built for Raleigh in 1587, and later sold to Queen Elizabeth.

TRINIDAD
Port of Spain
Go. Paria
Bo. Boca
Pedro Gallo
R. Orinoco
His First Voyage 1595
Kemys 1618
Mt. Aio 2nd Mine
St. Thome 1st Mine
Cataracts
R. Caroni

ATLANTIC
OCEAN

R. Esequibo
R. Berbice
R. Cressivo
R. Surinam
R. Cuyuni (Cayenne)

Second voyage, 1617-18

Imagined Lake of Manoa
EL DORADO
West 60° Longitude

60°   55°

10°   5°

F

CHAPTER THIRTEEN

GUIANA

The first action of the explorers was to attack the Spanish fort on Trinidad, St. Joseph, and take prisoner the governer, Antonio de Berreo. Raleigh, treating him with great courtesy, endeavoured to get him to talk about the route to El Dorado. It was a battle of wits, for Raleigh knew, by the intercepted letter, that Berreo was waiting for reinforcements from Spain to undertake that very journey. The Spaniard, on the whole, had the best of the discussion. He did not deny the existence of El Dorado; he merely warned Raleigh, in the most alarming and apparently sincere terms, of the appalling dangers of the quest, and besought him not to be so foolhardy; but he gave him no useful geographical hints.

Raleigh, however, had planned his journey to the south. Dividing Trinidad from the mainland of South America was a narrow strait, terrible in storm, known as the Serpent's Mouth. Emptying themselves into it were the many 'arms' of the Orinoco—'sixteen arms in all', as Raleigh described them—which made the coast a great delta composed of islands 'very great, many of them as big as the Isle of Wight and bigger'. Raleigh determined to cross the strait, to make his way down one of these tributaries to the Orinoco proper, to sail along it until he reached another great tributary which turned sharply south and led, so it was thought, to the great inland lake on whose shore stood El Dorado.

Such a journey was obviously impossible in the ships in which the expedition had crossed the Atlantic, and Raleigh prepared five boats of shallow draught to navigate the 'great river of Orenoque' (which Kemys loyally renamed and always referred to as 'the Raleana'). 'In the bottom of an old Galego', he wrote in his account of the expedition, 'which I caused to be fashioned like a galley, and in one barge, two wherries and a shipboat of *The Lion's Whelp*, we carried a hundred persons and their victuals for a month.' It was, indeed, an appalling voyage, for they were 'all driven to lie in the rain and weather, in the open air, in the burning sun, and upon the hard boards, and to dress our meat, and to carry all manner of furniture in them, wherewith they were so pestered and unsavoury that, what with the victuals being most fish, with wet clothes of so many men thrust together, and the heat of the sun, I will undertake there was never any prison in England that could be found more unsavoury and loathsome, especially to myself, who had for many years before been dieted and cared for in a sort far differing.'

After wasting some time in the maze of the delta, a captured Indian guided them to the tributary Amana whose fast-running, alligator-infested waters led them to the Orinoco. 'When three days more were overgone, our companies began to despair, the weather being extreme hot, the river being bordered with very high trees that kept away the air and the current against us every day stronger than other; but we evermore commanded our pilots to promise an end the next day and used it so long as we were driven to assure them from four reaches of the river to three, and so to two and so to the next reach; but so long we laboured as many days were spent and so driven to draw ourselves to harder allowance, our bread even to the last, and no drink at all, and our men and ourselves so wearied and scorched, and doubtful withal whether we should perform it or no, the heat increasing as we drew towards the line; for we were now in five degrees.'

On the fifteenth day, however, as they neared the main stream of the Orinoco the country opened out into a vision of an earthly paradise: 'On both sides of the river we passed the most beautiful country that mine eyes ever beheld . . . the grass short and green, and in divers parts groves of trees by themselves, as if they had been by all the art and labour in the world so made of purpose; and still as we rowed, the deer came down feeding by the water side, as if they had been used to a keeper's call.' But perhaps the most cheering sight was a basket of refiner's tools, which surely meant that gold could not be far off.

Once on the Orinoco, they—the first Englishmen to navigate it—saw far off the hills of Guiana which were their goal. The natives on the shores were hospitable. The King, Topiawari, 'came to us on foot from his house, which was fourteen English miles (himself being 110 years old) and returned on foot the same day and with him many of the borderers, with many women and children, that came to wonder at our nation and to bring us down victual, which they did in great plenty, as venison, pork, hens, chicken, fowl, fish, with divers sorts of excellent fruits and roots, and great abundance of *Pinas*, the princess of fruits'. The men got slightly drunk on the

juice of the pineapples; they were instructed by the natives in an antidote against poisoned arrows they might
later encounter; and Raleigh was given a pet—'a beast
called *Armadilla*, which seemeth to be all barred over with
small plates somewhat like to a *Renocero* with a white-
horn growing in the hinder parts, as big as a great hunt-
ing-horn, which they use to wind instead of a trumpet'.

Raleigh, on his side, explained to Topiawari (who
hated the Spaniards because they had treated his house and
tribe with great cruelty) that he was the 'servant of a
Queen who was the great cacique (chief) of the north and
a virgin' who was the enemy of the Spaniards and 'having
freed all the coast of the northern world from their servi-
tude had sent me to free them also, and withal to defend
the country of Guiana from their invasion and conquest'.
Topiawari thereupon made an alliance with him and
offered to journey with him to El Dorado, if he would
leave behind fifty of his men to protect the tribe against a
possible assault of Spaniards. This, however, Raleigh
could not do. Nor, since the season was now late and the
Orinoco would soon be rising, with its accompanying
storms, could he press on into the heart of the fabled
Manoa. His men, too, declared they could no longer row
against the current which was so strong that 'we were not
able with a barge of eight oars to row one stone's cast in
an hour'. But he would take an overland expedition,
accompanied by Topiawari's only son, Caworako, to gain
a view of the Promised Land and to assure himself of the
presence of gold.

'When we were come to the tops of the first hills of the
plains adjoining to the river, we beheld that wonderful
breach of waters which ran down Caroli: and might from

that mountain see the river, how it ran in three parts, above twenty miles off; and there appeared some ten or twelve overfalls in sight, every one as high above the other as a Church tower, which fell with that fury that the rebound of water made it seem as if it had been all covered over with a great shower of rain; and in some places we took it at first for a smoke that had risen over some great town. For mine own part I was well persuaded from thence to have returned, being a very ill footman; but the rest were all so desirous to go near the said strange thunder of waters as they drew me on little by little till we came into the next valley where we might better discern the same.'

They were rewarded for their perseverance. 'I never saw a more beautiful country, nor more lively prospects; hills so raised here and there over the valleys; the river winding into divers branches; the plains adjoining without bush or stubble, all fair green grass: the ground of hard sand easy to march on, either for foot or horse; the deer crossing in every path; the birds towards the evening singing in every tree with a thousand several tunes; cranes and herons of white, crimson and carnation perching in the river's side; the air fresh, with a gentle easterly wind; and every stone that we stooped to take up promised either gold or silver by his complexion . . . and yet we had no means but our daggers and fingers to tear them out here and there, the rocks being most hard of that mineral Spar, which is like a flint and is altogether as hard or harder, and besides, the veins like a fathom or two deep in the rocks.'

But they must go home. Orinoco was rising. 'All the night it was stormy and dark, and full of thunder and great showers ... we were heartily afraid both of the billow and terrible current.' They left behind them two of their company, Francis Sparrow, to sketch the country, and a boy, Hugh Godwin, to learn the language, and eventually, after much peril by water, came to Trinidad again, 'where we found our ships at anchor, than which there was never to us a more joyful sight'.

Six weeks later, in the August of 1595, they were in England once more.

CHAPTER FOURTEEN

THE FRUITS OF DISCOVERY

The forty-three-year-old Raleigh who returned from Guiana was, by his own description, 'a beggar and withered'. He had brought back not a cargo of gold, but a few samples of ore and tales of a possible empire. These were not only insufficient to purchase his pardon but they actually diminished his credit. He was not believed. During his seven months' absence, the malice of his enemies had been unsleeping and now they circulated the report in court and city that he was a liar and a cheat. He had not in fact ever left Cornwall; the ores he had brought home had been mined in the West Country; his indubitably American souvenirs had been taken from a Spanish prize-ship, whose capture he had not disclosed; and his reminiscences were mere travellers' tales that anyone could pick up.

It was partly to answer these calumnies that he wrote his *Discovery of the Large, Rich and Beautiful Empire of Guiana*, a small book of 112 pages, which appeared the following year, immediately became a best-seller and is still one of the best travel books in the English language. The sceptics were still sceptical and Raleigh, in places, gave them some reason for it, for he reported not only what he himself had seen and done, but what he had been told. Topiawari's tribe, for example, had told him of another tribe 'whose heads appear not above their shoulders. . . . They are called Ewaipanoma; they are reported to have their eyes in their shoulders and their mouths in the middle of their breasts, and that a long train of hair groweth backward between the shoulders.' Shakespeare, who to the end of his life continued his literary vendetta against Raleigh, used this particular incredibility both in *Othello*—

> *The Anthropophagi and men whose heads*
> *Do grow beneath their shoulders*

and, more bitterly, in *The Tempest*—

>   *such men*
> *Whose head stood in their breasts—which now we find*
> *Each putter-out of five for one will bring us*
> *Good warrant of,*

—a pointed sneer at such expeditions as Raleigh's.

Paradoxically, it was in English literature that the results of the discovery of Guiana were to be found. Despite Shakespeare's hostility, *The Tempest* is haunted by it and Caliban himself, as one critic has pointed out, 'is surely a representation of the primitive races spoken of by Raleigh'. On Milton, in his descriptions of Eden and in his love for sonorous-sounding names, Raleigh's influence is even more obvious. One may compare Raleigh's 'Guiana, and that great and golden city, which the Spaniards call El Dorado, and the naturals Manoa, which city was conquered, re-edified and enlarged by a younger son of Guianacapa, Emperor of Peru, at such time as Francisco Pizarro and others conquered the said empire from his two elder brethren, Guascar and Atabalipa, both then

contending for the same, the one being favoured by the
Orejones of Cuzco', with Milton's:

> *Rich Mexico, the seat of Montezume,*
> *And Cuzco in Peru, the richer seat*
> *Of Atabalipa, and yet unspoiled*
> *Guiana, whose great city Geryon's sons*
> *Call El Dorado.*

And some have seen the magic extend even to Bunyan,
whose Land of Beaulah recalls the plains and hills of
Guiana and whose Shining Ones 'inhabit a City yet more
splendid than Manoa'.

At the time, Chapman himself wrote his best poem on
the actual expedition—*De Guiana Carmen Epicum*—in
which he acclaims Raleigh as the soul of England:

> *O how most like*
> *Art thou, heroic author of this act,*
> *To this wronged soul of Nature, that sustain'st*
> *Pain, charge and peril for thy country's good,*
> *And she, much like a body marred with surfeits,*
> *Feels not . . .*

and sees the venture not merely as a quest for gold but as
Marlowe, had he lived, might have seen it, as a 'spiritual
achievement of Tamburlaine's kind'—a thrusting out into
the unknown by valiant spirits who preferred risking
death in action to the living death of frustration:

> *You know that Death lives where power lives unus'd*

and, renouncing 'the prison'd life of beasts', became—

> *You that herein renounce the course of earth*
> *And lift your eyes for guidance to the stars.*

But neither Chapman's poetry nor Raleigh's prose
could move the Queen. Raleigh might expatiate on the
new country 'that hath yet her maidenhead, never sacked,
turned nor wrought, the face of the earth hath not been
torn, nor the virtue and the salt of the soil spent by man-
urance, the graves have not been opened for gold, the
mines not broken with sledges, nor their images pulled
down out of their temples. It hath never been entered by
any army of strength and never conquered or possessed
by any Christian prince.' He might write angrily to her
in a letter: 'If the Spaniards had been so blockish and
slothful, we had not feared now their power, who by
their gold from thence vex and endanger all the estates of
kings.' Chapman might remind her that

> Guiana, whose rich seat are mines of gold,
> Whose forehead knocks against the roof of stars,
>   Stands on her tiptoes, at fair England looking,
> Kissing her hand, bowing her mighty breast,
>   And every sign of all submission making,
> To be her sister and her daughter both,
> Of our most sacred Maid.

and implore her to:

> Go forth upon the waters, and create
> A golden world in this our iron age.

Elizabeth would not move. She was old and the great
days had gone. Frobisher, Hawkins, Drake were all dead
now. In her ear little 'dwarf Cecil' whispered caution and
Essex dropped poison about Raleigh. She would not even
consider his alternative plan of making an alliance with
Guiana, sending merely a small protective and mining

force. Raleigh, at his own expense, sent Kemys out again to keep what contacts he had made; but he himself was kept kicking his heels at Sherborne, still debarred from Court and employment, and finding what relief he could in sea-bathing at Weymouth or in taking the waters at Bath.

CHAPTER FIFTEEN

CADIZ

The year 1596 saw a financial crisis in England. For two successive years the rain had spoilt the harvests and food prices had soared to famine heights. People were dying in the streets; there were riots and turbulent men crying out that 'they must not starve, they will not starve'. They cried out too against the continuing war with Spain, with its drain of men and money. Yet peace was impossible, for that spring there were reports of a new Spanish Armada in the Channel. As a desperate measure, which if successful might both cripple Spain and replenish the English exchequer, Elizabeth at last sanctioned the strategy which, for years, her sea-dogs had been urging on her—to attack Spain's chief port, Cadiz, and capture the entire treasure fleet in harbour there. For such an exploit, whatever her private feelings might be, Raleigh was needed. He was the last of the great seamen and, in Spanish eyes at least, the heir of Drake—the notorious English pirate 'Guateral', who had recently, 'after having caused much trouble and injury to the Isle of Trinidad and its inhabitants', entered the Orinoco. In the spring of 1596 Raleigh was ordered to co-operate with Essex on the Cadiz project.

His task was not easy. The Court, flattering the reigning favourite, blamed the fallen one for any delays and hindrances that might occur. When he failed to appear at Plymouth they said that 'his slackness and stay by the way is not thought to be upon sloth or negligence, but upon pregnant design'—an interpretation elaborated by one of Essex's friends who wrote of 'there being no kind of news of Sir Walter Raleigh, whose stay seemed to stay all and to put the Earl of Essex to insupportable charges'. Raleigh was, as a matter of fact, trying to collect crews. 'As fast as we press men one day, they come away another and say that they will not serve,' he wrote to Cecil. 'I cannot write to our generals at this time; for the poursevant found me in a country village, a mile from Gravesend, hunting after runaway mariners, and dragging in the mire from alehouse to alehouse.'

When at last he joined them at Plymouth he behaved with utmost tact, and treated Essex in a way which an observer, naturally seeing him as the Fox, described as 'the cunningest respect and deepest humility that ever I saw'. But he was, after all, only Rear-Admiral, and he had no doubt that it was necessity rather than choice which made him even that. Supreme command was vested jointly in Lord Howard, as veteran of the Armada, and Essex, as the Favourite; Howard's nephew, Lord Thomas Howard, was Vice-Admiral, and Sir Francis Vere the first soldier in England but a bitter enemy of Raleigh, was in command of the troops.

The expedition, consisting of ninety-six ships and about 14,000 men (of whom 6,500 were soldiers) and accompanied by a Dutch contingent of twenty-four ships and about 2,500 men, was divided into four squadrons, led by the elder Howard on the *Ark Royal*, Essex on the *Repulse*, the younger Howard on the *Merhonour* and Ral-

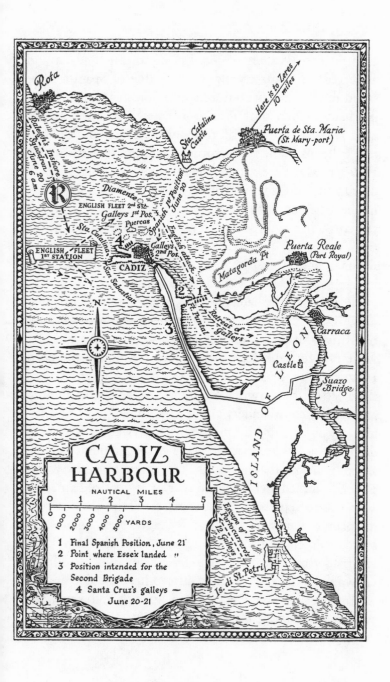

Rota

Here is to Zeres
10 miles

Sta. Catalina
Castle

Puerta de Sta. Maria
(St. Mary-port)

Raleigh's Inshore
Squadron
June 6 a.m.

R

Diamente

ENGLISH FLEET 2ND STN.
Galleys 1ST Pos.
Puercas

*Spanish 1st Position
June 20*

Sta. Catalina

ENGLISH FLEET
1ST STATION

4

Galleys
2ND Pos.

English attack

Puerta Reale
(Port Royal)

CADIZ

San Sebastian

2 1

Matagorda Pt.

3

*Retreat of
galleys*

Castle

Carraca

*Suazo
Bridge*

N

ISLAND OF LEON

CADIZ
HARBOUR

NAUTICAL MILES

0   1   2   3   4   5

1000 2000 3000 4000 5000 YARDS

1 Final Spanish Position, June 21
2 Point where Essex landed   "
3 Position intended for the
   Second Brigade
4 Santa Cruz's galleys —
   June 20-21

*Escape of
Porto carrero's
12 galleys*

Is. di St. Petri

eigh on the *Warspite*. It left Plymouth on June 1st and appeared off Cadiz on the 22nd. A line of Spanish ships sailed out of the harbour and stood on guard. The English held a Council of War, but Raleigh was not present at it. He had been sent off to scour the coast for any fugitive galleons. When he returned he found that Essex, the Howards and Vere had decided to make a military attack on the city of Cadiz instead of a naval attack on the fleet in the harbour. They were endeavouring to disembark the crews in a wild sea; men and boats were sinking; the troops were in dismay. Raleigh arrived at the critical moment and, from that moment he became in fact, if not in name, the leader of the 'Cadiz action'.

He went immediately to Essex and pointed out that these insane tactics meant 'our general ruin, to the utter overthrow of the whole armies, their own lives and Her Majesty's future safety'. Essex laid the blame on Lord Howard who, he said, 'would not consent to enter with the fleet till the town were first possessed' but, finding among the commanders about him a unanimity of criticism of an attempted landing where 'twenty men in so desperate a descent would have defeated them all', he asked Raleigh to endeavour to reason with Howard. Raleigh immediately went to that sixty-year-old amateur who was so depressed by the spectacle of the obvious ruin his plan was entailing that at Raleigh's request he consented to countermand the order. As Raleigh in his ship returned from the Lord Admiral, Essex and his officers crowded to the side of their ship to hear the decision.

'*Entramos*,' shouted Raleigh in Spanish and Essex answered by flinging his hat into the sea. Both Raleigh's cry and Essex's gesture have now become a legend but, divorced from their context, their meaning has been lost. What Raleigh announced was his own leadership. It was on Raleigh's advice that the fleet now moved up to the mouth of the harbour and it was Raleigh who, at ten o'clock that night, wrote out his plan of action and sent it to Lord Howard.

Next morning he was, as the architect of the attack, given the place of honour in leading the assault. Seventeen galleons lay under the walls of Cadiz, ready to close on the English fleet once it had entered the harbour through the narrow bottleneck and cut off its retreat. 'There was also a fort called the *Philip*, which beat and commanded the harbour. There were also ordnance, which lay all along the curtain upon the wall towards the sea. There were also divers other pieces of culverin, which also scoured the channel.' Into this massed fire Raleigh in the *Warspite* led the *Mary Rose*, the *Lion*, the *Rainbow*, the *Swiftsure*, the *Dreadnought*, the *Nonpareil*, with 'the twelve ships of London' and flyboats for boarding. And, as the cannonade broke, he replied with perhaps the most magnificent of his gestures. He held his fire and replied to the Spanish shots by ironical blasts of trumpets.

His immediate objective was 'the *St. Philip*, the great and famous Admiral of Spain', on whose decks his cousin Grenville had died. And no one in the action that day, either Spaniard or Englishman, needed the explanation which he gave in his account of the battle—that he was 'resolved to be revenged for the *Revenge* or to second her with mine own life'.

Essex, meanwhile, 'being impatient to abide far off, hearing so great a thunder of ordnance, thrust up through the fleet' and came close to Raleigh. The general battle now commenced. For three hours they attacked the Spaniards and 'the volleys of cannon and culverin came as thick as if it had been a skirmish of musketeers'. At last Raleigh, badly battered, saw that if he was not to sink he must board the *St. Philip* and, having by then no flyboats, went in his skiff to Essex to ask for some. In the actual companionship of fighting the two men, as always, forgot their differences and only remembered each other's courage. Essex promised 'he would second me in person, on his honour'.

While Raleigh was away from his ship talking to Essex, Vere in the *Rainbow*, and Lord Thomas Howard in the *Nonpareil*, pushed ahead of the *Warspite* and so gained the place of honour in the lead. Raleigh, on his return, made the third of his remembered gestures. He had given the word '*Entramos*'; he had replied to cannon-fire with trumpets; now he nosed through his two rivals and, having gained the lead, swung the *Warspite* athwart the narrowest part of the channel 'so I was sure that none should outstart me again for that day'. Even the flyboats could not get through, so Raleigh 'laid out a warp by the side of the *Philip* to shake hands with her'. But the Spaniards did not wait for the boarding. They ran the ship aground and fled 'tumbling into the sea heaps of soldiers, so thick as if coals had been poured out of a sack in many ports at once, some drowned and some sticking in the mud'. Before leaving the ship they fired it and the victors saw 'so huge a fire and such tearing of the ordnance in the great *Philip*, and the rest, when the fire came to them as, if any man had a desire to see Hell itself, it was there most lively figured'. The *Revenge* was revenged.

The Spanish fleet defeated, the English army was now

put ashore to attack the town which 'was carried with a sudden fury and with little loss'. Raleigh entered it only for a moment. Towards the end of the sea-battle he was wounded, his leg being 'interlaced and deformed with splinters', but he insisted on being taken ashore on the shoulders of his men and even attempted to ride a horse. But the pain was too agonizing. Also there was actual danger for one in his condition from 'the tumultuous, disordered soldiers that, being then given over to spoil and rapine, had no respect'. He returned to the fleet, which was almost deserted—everyone, from the admirals downwards, 'running headlong to the sack'.

He spent the night on his ship, lamed for life, while others gained the spoils of his strategy.

CHAPTER SIXTEEN

THE QUEEN IS NOT PLEASED

Throughout the night the looting and burning of Cadiz continued. At daybreak, Raleigh sent his half-brother and his brother-in-law, Sir John Gilbert and Arthur Throckmorton, to beg leave of Lord Howard to go into the Puerto Real roads and seize the merchant ships. The capture of these, worth twelve million crowns, was, after all, one of the main objects of the expedition. Howard was as much aware of this as Raleigh, but as practically the entire fleet was engaged in procuring its own portable treasures from Cadiz, there was no one to send. 'The confusion was great; it was almost impossible to order many things at once.' So Raleigh's request was refused.

The forty ships, bottled up in the bay of which the English commanded the entrance, could not escape and, during the day, as they were still untouched, the merchants of Cadiz offered to ransom them for two million ducats. This Howard refused, remarking: 'We came to consume them, not to compound with them.' He was willing to consider an offer for the merchandise, but he insisted on claiming the ships themselves as prizes. Raleigh urged that they should seize them first and argue afterwards. The debate went on through the night. Next morning the Spanish Admiral, the Duke of Medina Sidonia, solved their problem for them. He burnt them, ships, merchandise and all.

On the Sunday a great service of thanksgiving was held in Cadiz, followed by a banquet, at which Essex and Howard made sixty-six knights—more, as a contemporary wrote, than had ever existed in England before. 'The honour never recovered from the degradation it suffered on that occasion', and the ballad-makers of the time sang of:

> *A Gentleman of Wales, with a Knight of Cales*
> (Cadiz)
> *And a laird of the North Countree—*
> *A yeoman of Kent upon a racked rent*
> *Could buy them out all three.*

Next day another Council of War was held at which it was decided that Raleigh and Lord Thomas Howard should take sufficient ships to capture the treasure fleet now believed to be crossing the Atlantic, while Lord Howard on the flagship, accompanied by Essex, should return to England with the damaged ships and the sick men. Essex upset this plan by announcing that he was now Governor of Cadiz and intended to stay there. Howard refused to sail without him. The deadlock was resolved by a decision to return home all together in leisurely fashion, making what raids and inroads they could by the way. The only thing they captured of any lasting value was the library of Bishop Osorius, which they secured during a raid on Faro and which was eventually given to Oxford, where it became the nucleus of the Bodleian Library.

The Queen, in spite of her care for learning, did not

consider this as an equivalent of the treasure she had anti-
cipated. She was furious at the loss of the treasure ships, at
the personal looting by army and navy alike of what
should have been added to the national revenue, at the
sixty-six rag-tag-and-bobtail knights. She 'resolved that
the service at Cadiz should be no matter for reward or
distinction to anybody' and even refused to allow the
general thanksgiving for victory which had been arranged
throughout the country to be celebrated anywhere outside London.

There were, however, factors beyond her control. The
victory at Cadiz did, in fact, ensure England's supremacy
at sea and her rise in international importance to match
Spain's decline. It has been justly described as the Elizabethan Trafalgar. It established Elizabeth's reputation in
Europe. In Venice, for example, they demanded a picture
of her, saying: 'Great is the Queen of England! O, what
a woman if she were but a Christian!' It caught the
imagination of contemporaries even more than the defensive action against the Armada, of which it might be
considered the complement and completion. And the
populace attributed it all to Essex. With his genius for
courting the crowd, Essex lodged himself irremovably in
the country's affection and became, after Cadiz, as powerful a name to conjure with as was Nelson's memory after
Trafalgar.

As for Raleigh, he had reversed many men's verdict on
him even if he had not been able to influence the Queen's.
One of his erstwhile detractors wrote: 'Sir Walter Raleigh did in my judgment, no man better; and his artillery
most effect. I never knew the gentleman until this time,
and I am sorry for it, for there are in him excellent things

beside his valour.' A correspondent wrote to Robert Cecil, summing the matter up: 'Sir Walter Raleigh's service was so much praiseworthy as those which were formerly his enemies do now hold him in great estimation.' Yet there was no immediate return to favour. This was in the end brought about by the diplomacy of Cecil and the neutrality, if not the encouragement, of Essex, who, with the changing needs and policies of a reign obviously drawing to its end, saw certain advantages in a triumvirate of themselves and Raleigh.

Gradually, from the opening of 1597, men noticed 'the Fox's' rehabilitation. He was, during February, in constant conference with Essex. By April he was noted to be 'daily at Court' and hopeful of returning to his position with the Queen. On June 1st he was officially forgiven. Elizabeth 'used him graciously and gave him full authority to execute his place as Captain of the Guard, which he immediately undertook, and swore many men into the places void'. That evening he was on duty at her side again, more ostentatiously magnificent than ever in a new suit of silver armour.

CHAPTER SEVENTEEN

SIR ROBERT CECIL

On the same day as the Cadiz fleet sailed Queen Elizabeth had made Sir Robert Cecil, Burleigh's second son, her Secretary—a post carrying with it far more power then than that of Prime Minister in later centuries. He was thirty-three—eleven years younger than Raleigh, three years older than Essex—and from that moment until his death sixteen years later, he was the real ruler of England. As long as Elizabeth lived his power was uncertain, but after the accession of James I (who owed the English throne to Cecil's manoeuvres) he was immovably secure.

He was a dwarf and a hunchback, splay-footed, already grey-haired, constantly ill, usually overworked. He had been trained by his father in statecraft and, from an early age was master of the science of using and directing for his own ends men's weakness and ambition. Falsehood had become so second nature with him that he was unable to speak the truth even to his own friends. Machiavelli could have taught him nothing and it was he, not Raleigh, who was the real English 'Machiavel'. By the side of him, Raleigh (who was related to him by marriage) and Essex (who had been brought up as his playmate, companion and foster-brother) were not the two Machiavellian types, the Fox and the Lion. They were more like

two frisking lambs in the presence of a wolf. It is a tribute
to his matchless dissimulation that neither of them realized it until it was too late. To consolidate his power during the last uneasy years of Elizabeth's reign, Cecil needed
both Essex's popularity with the country and Raleigh's
courage and ability. (It is probable that he never forgot
the object lesson which Raleigh had given him when he
went down to Devon to restore order at the looting of
the Carrack.) But he naturally allowed both of them to
suppose that they were using him.

If he was capable of affection for any human being but
himself, he felt it for his young wife who died at the beginning of 1597. Raleigh's letter to him on this occasion,
which bound them together in a genuine sorrow, was
characteristic of the writer: 'You have lost a good and
virtuous wife and myself an honourable friend and kins-
woman. But there was a time when she was unknown to
you, for whom you then lamented not. She is now no
more yours, nor of your acquaintance, but immortal, and
not needing or knowing your love or sorrow. Therefore
you shall but grieve for that which now is as then it was
when not yours; only bettered by the difference in this,
that she hath passed the wearisome journey of this dark
world and hath possession of her inheritance. . . .

'I believe that sorrows are dangerous companions, con-
verting bad into evil and evil in worse, and do no other
service than multiply harms. They are the treasures of
weak hearts and of the foolish. The mind that entertaineth
them is as the earth and dust whereon sorrows and adversities of the world do, as the beasts of the field, tread,
trample and defile. The mind of man is that part of God
which is in us which, by how much it is subject to passion

by so much it is farther from him that gave it us. Sorrows draw not the dead to life, but the living to death. . . .'

Nor was Raleigh's sympathy only in words. He and his wife took a special interest in Cecil's motherless son, Will, who stayed with them in the country air of Sherborne to recuperate under Lady Raleigh's motherly attention and to study under Raleigh's direction. 'His stomach, that was heretofore weak, is altogether amended', wrote Raleigh to Cecil three years later, 'and he doth now eat well and digest rightly. I hope this air will agree exceedingly with him. He is also better kept to his book than anywhere else.'

There was thus between Raleigh and Cecil what, with anyone less cold-blooded than the little Secretary, would be considered genuine friendship. And on Raleigh's side it seems to have lasted in a curious way even after Cecil by his machinations had finally ruined him.

But in 1597 there was no cleavage between them. The return to favour, the friendliness of Essex, the good offices of Cecil must have seemed to Raleigh like a new dawn. The three grew 'exceedingly great' together, according to the gossips, and were constantly 'very private' at Cecil's house. In the July of 1597 they saw together a performance of Shakespeare's new play, *Richard II*, after which Raleigh wrote to Cecil that Essex was 'wonderful merry at your conceit of Richard the Second. I hope it shall never alter, and thereof I shall be most glad of, as the true way to all our good, quiet and advancement, and most of all for Her sake whose affairs shall hereby find better progression.'

No one has been able satisfactorily to interpret this cryptic remark. In Raleigh's mind, whatever was decided was obviously for the Queen's benefit, and this must have been Cecil's ostensible purpose. Yet may not the mimic performance of the deposing of a sovereign have sown a seed in the mind of the unstable and ambitious Essex? Four years later, on the eve of his rebellion, it was, at his request, performed again, and one of the charges against him at his trial was that he had watched it. This may not have been Cecil's intention; but it is a perfect example of the Cecilian method.

Whatever lay behind it, this occasion was the last on which the three met in unclouded amity. Five days later Raleigh and Essex sailed together on a new expedition, leaving Cecil to guard their interests with the Queen.

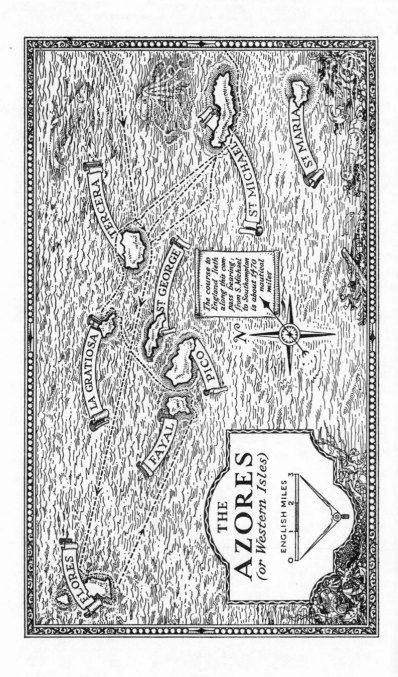

ST MARIA

ST MICHAEL

TERCERA

ST GEORGE

The course to
England lieth
along this com-
pass bearing;
from S. Michael
to Southampton
is about 1470
nautical
miles

LA GRATIOSA

PICO

FAYAL

FLORES

THE
AZORES
(or Western Isles)

ENGLISH MILES
0   1   2   3

CHAPTER EIGHTEEN

THE ISLANDS VOYAGE

The new expedition was planned on the same lines as the Cadiz action. Spain was preparing to avenge that disaster and was building a new Armada in the port of Ferrol. Ferrol was therefore to be captured, as Cadiz had been, and the work in progress destroyed. And, as a sequel to the main action, the West Indian silver fleet of the year was to be taken. The higher command was the same as before, except that Lord Howard had at last retired, leaving Essex alone as Lord Admiral, with Lord Thomas Howard and Raleigh in their previous positions as Vice-Admiral and Rear-Admiral.

The fleet sailed from Plymouth on July 10th, but was driven back by a violent storm which did so much damage that it was not ready to restart until August 17th. For various reasons, the attack on Ferrol had now become impracticable and it was decided to sail to the Azores to concentrate on the capture of the treasure fleet. Again gales broke up the expedition before it eventually gathered together at Flores to settle the plan of campaign. The strategy had to take account of the fact that the island of Terceira was too strongly fortified to be successfully attacked and so offered a safe anchorage to the Spanish fleet, if only it could reach it. One of the smaller islands must thus be occupied by the English to serve as a base from which to attack the silver fleet before it could make Terceira. The island decided on was Fayal, to which Essex sailed, leaving Raleigh at Flores to finish watering his ships but with instructions to follow him to Fayal immediately this necessary but slow operation was finished.

When Raleigh arrived at Fayal, Essex was not there. He had gone off on one of his wild-goose chases. For two days Raleigh waited, ignoring the firing from the fort, the digging of entrenchments, the hanging out of a flag of defiance and the evacuation to the interior. On the third day he held a Council of War, and in spite of the protests of the Essex faction, led by Sir Gelly Merrick (Essex's steward, whom he had knighted at Cadiz), he determined to attack. Merrick refused to participate in an action which would rob his patron of the glory and withdrew his six ships. Raleigh, with five hundred picked men, all of them sailors (including the faithful Kemys as a volunteer), landed and, leading them in no armour but a collar, made himself master of both the fort and the town.

Next day Essex arrived. His faction, led by Merrick, urged him to court martial Raleigh and execute him for breach of orders. That this would have been possible both Raleigh and Essex knew, and when at last Raleigh met him, it was as 'the Fox' that he had to behave. Essex charged him with having contravened the order forbidding the landing of troops without permission. Raleigh pointed out that the order applied to a 'Captain or military officer' and therefore did not apply to him.

'I take myself to be a principal commander, under your Lordship, and therefore not subject to that Article, nor under the power of the law martial', he said, 'because a successive commander of the whole fleet in Her Majesty's

Letters Patent, your Lordship and my Lord Thomas Howard failing.'

Essex accepted the defence, but insisted that no mention should be made of Raleigh's exploit in the official despatch and refused to sup with him as a token of restored amity. Raleigh, mistrusting what might happen, decided to stay with his own squadron and, if necessary, fight Essex if he made an attempt to arrest him; but Lord Thomas Howard intervened and a reconciliation was patched up.

Essex decided to outshine Raleigh and to capture St. Michael's Island. He ordered the whole fleet to follow him, with the result that 'three hours later the long-sought Flota, one of the richest ever to leave the West Indies, cut across the wash of the English squadrons'. Before Essex could return, the silver fleet was safely in harbour in Terceira and the treasure in the vaults of the impregnable fortress. Essex thereupon decided to try to storm the fort, but the odds were so obviously hopeless that the dissuasions of Raleigh and Lord Thomas Howard were successful in preventing what would have been a massacre.

The English fleet now had nothing to do but to return home, having failed to accomplish anything it set out to do. But worse was to come. By not attacking the new Armada at Ferrol, Essex had laid England open to invasion. On the same day that the English began their return from the 'Islands Voyage', the Spanish sailed—one hundred and thirty-six ships bent on revenge and conquest. The panic which reigned in England was far greater than that in 1588, for this time there was no fleet to defend the coasts. Further, that fleet itself was straggling home in a leisurely manner, quite unaware of the enemy lying in wait for it. What saved both the country and the fleet was the weather—the gale which blew crippling the new Armada and delaying Essex's return. When, eventually, the errant expedition reached England, having nothing to report but three small captured ships that hardly paid expenses, Elizabeth was even more angry than usual.

CHAPTER NINETEEN

RALEIGH RETURNS TO FAVOUR

The final estrangement of Essex and the Queen dates from the return from the Islands Voyage. Elizabeth understood what had happened. During his absence she had made old Lord Howard Earl of Nottingham, with the result that he now took precedence of Essex. Essex stormed and sulked till the whole Court was in a turmoil, and then retired to his country seat on the excuse that he was ill. It was Raleigh who healed the breach by suggesting to the Queen that Essex's precedence should be restored by making him Earl Marshal. Essex came back to Court and, apparently, to favour. But it was never to be the same again.

For the remaining five years of the reign Raleigh occupied once more the dominant place at Court; though he wore the Favouriteship with a difference. Lame, worn with his voyages, disillusioned, he seemed far older than his forty-six years. When Burleigh died in 1598 he alone was left of the figures of the great days, and this loneliness of itself bound him and the Queen together in their memories and understanding. Yet if he now occupied a place in some ways comparable to that which Leicester had once held, he had also to take account of the realities of the changing age. Essex was still the idol of the country and, spasmodically, by virtue of his overwhelming charm when he cared to exercise it, the spoilt darling of the Queen. Cecil had stepped coldly into his father's shoes and his concurrence was as necessary as ever Burleigh's had been. The triumvirate was still essential to them all, though events—not unaided by Cecil's statecraft—rapidly brought about the first phase of its dissolution, aligning Raleigh and Cecil against Essex.

Against this background, Raleigh's day-to-day activities continued to exhibit his energy and versatility. As Member of Parliament, he was prominent in the sessions of 1597 and 1598, defending free speech, discussing economic policy in regard to the Queen's debts, speaking now on the subject of beggars who pretended that they had been ruined by the wars, now on the rights of the Lower House against the Upper on points of ceremonial respect. He advised on defence and urged a 'strong' policy on Ireland where rebellion had once more broken out.

He was made Governor of Jersey and won gratitude and respect from the islanders by his wise administration. He was appointed to welcome and entertain Henri IV's Minister, Sully, on his official visit to England. In the West Country he supported the tin-miners in their struggle against the Corporation of Plymouth and busied himself with the administration of the Duchy. His interest in Guiana and Virginia never flagged—his pinnace, the *Wat* (named after his son), reached Guiana in 1597—and among other things he imported cedar and sassafras wood for Sherborne. There life went quietly and uneventfully on, a haven of refuge against the storms of Court.

Here he remained as Captain of the Guard, for in spite of his wisdom and authority, he was not made Privy Councillor. In the summer of 1598 Cecil promised to try to procure him that post whose functions he had so often exercised, and there were rumours that he was also to be made Vice-Chamberlain. But it came to nothing and the Irish situation, combined with the final rupture of the triumvirate and a public breach with Essex, postponed any consideration of it.

In the·August of 1598 Tyrone routed an English force on the Blackwater, 'the greatest loss and dishonour the Queen hath had in her time', and the matter of Ireland became of immediate significance. Essex naturally saw a chance of getting Raleigh involved in Ireland (it cannot have escaped the memory of either of them that Raleigh's absences in Ireland had coincided with Essex's greatest favour at home) and, as Raleigh had withdrawn his own name from the list of possible Lord Deputies, he urged the appointment of one of Raleigh's relations and partisans. When Elizabeth refused, he turned his back on her and she boxed his ears. He then rushed from the room and retired, 'ill' again, to Wanstead.

The Queen eventually grew tired of his malingering and remarked that she intended 'to stand as much upon her greatness as he hath done upon his stomach'. In the autumn he decided to apologize and return to Court. He chose the occasion carefully. There was to be a tournament on the Queen's Accession Day. Hearing that Raleigh, as Captain of the Guard, intended to bring his followers in orange-plumed hats and orange favours, he mustered his own considerable faction—the knights he had made, his retainers and other servants, up to the number of two thousand men, appearing as a private army—and insisted on their wearing the same. By this means he thought to make Raleigh look ridiculous. Unfortunately, the Queen considered the joke was directed against her and she made her displeasure obvious by terminating the proceedings. The eventual sequel was that it was Essex who was sent to Ireland as Lord Deputy.

The country, of course, saw this appointment in a very different light. The populace were still too dazzled by the Earl to notice the catastrophic truth about his leadership. His opposition to the hated Raleigh had increased his popularity; and even his disfavour with Elizabeth had gained him new allies in the Puritans, who saw him as the victim of the worldly wickedness of the Court.

His appointment as Lord Deputy, charged with the subjugation of Ireland, thus seemed to the people not only an appropriate but a necessary step. A popular ballot, had such a thing been imagined, would have procured the same result. Shakespeare, producing a patriotic play for the occasion, *Henry V*, introduced a reference which could not fail to draw applause—a veritable clap-trap:

> *Were now the general of our gracious empress*
> *(As in good time he may) from Ireland coming,*
> *Bringing rebellion broached on his sword,*
> *How many would the peaceful city quit*
> *To welcome him!*

But Essex himself knew the realities of the situation. In spite of the fact that he had been given an army such as had never been taken to Ireland before; in spite of the enormous powers allowed him—'so ample a Commission as might give his ambition full power', he was haunted by the thought of Raleigh at home, dropping poison in the Queen's ear as he, when the positions had been reversed, had dropped it. In a revealing letter to the Queen he asked: 'Is it not lamented by your Majesty's faithfullest subjects, both here and there, that a Cobham[1] and Raleigh should have such credit and favour with your Majesty when they wish the ill success of your Majesty's most important action, the decay of your greatest strength, and the destruction of your faithfullest servants?' Even had Raleigh wished this, there was no need for him to have moved. Essex's own incompetence was sufficient to compass his downfall.

[1] Cecil's brother-in-law.

CHAPTER TWENTY

THE END OF ESSEX

The Irish campaign was a failure. Essex knighted another seventy or so of his followers; wasted time and men in pointless skirmishes and eventually in contravention of orders made an ignominious truce with Tyrone. He then hurried home and, without waiting to change from his journey, rode straight to Elizabeth (who was at Nonsuch) and burst into her room before she had finished her toilet.

'God's Death, my Lord,' she said. 'What do you here, your presence hateful without Tyrone's head?' and ordered him from the room because 'his boots stunk'. That evening he was placed under house arrest and shortly afterwards in the custody of the Lord Keeper. He was compelled to admit his misdeeds to the Council on his knees, and his main source of wealth was taken from him by the Queen's refusal to renew his monopoly of sweet wines.

The country was in a ferment. Essex's followers, crossing from Ireland, whipped up a discontent which needed no stimulant. The sweet-wine issue, in its effect on the populace, was second only to that of the Armada. The popularity of Essex—and, in consequence, the unpopularity of Raleigh—reached a new peak, which encouraged the Earl when he was released from his imprisonment, to risk a *coup d'état*. He would raise London, capture the Palace and rescue the Queen from her 'evil Counsellors'. Raleigh should die. In the event it was Essex who died.

The story of Essex's rebellion belongs, in its fullness, to the history of England. But if here we are concerned only with Raleigh's part in it, that part is really the key to the whole. For, in Essex's mind it was against Raleigh that the whole project was directed. In the minds of Essex's partisans, then and since, it was Raleigh who secured Essex's execution. The truth seems to be that Essex, ever since the Islands Voyage, had allowed his hatred of Raleigh to become an obsession which approached insanity and, since the Queen's snub at the tournament, had realized that his rival could only be removed by force. Raleigh, on his part, was quite willing to destroy Essex, but the circumstances of the time made the duel not merely what it had been in the earlier days, a matter of Court rivalry, but a constitutional issue. By his position, Raleigh, merely by defending himself, was also defending the Crown; Essex for the same reason was attacking it. And, at the back was Cecil, using Raleigh for the destruction of Essex until the time should be ready for him to destroy Raleigh and erect on the ruins of the triumvirate his own dictatorship.

The first move in the mortal struggle was made even before Essex returned from Ireland. On 9th August 1599 the fleet was once more put in readiness against a rumoured attack from Spain. Raleigh and Lord Thomas Howard went down to take command and London was barricaded. The danger, however, was (as they knew) not from Spain (as it was announced to the populace) but from Essex. It was feared that he intended to use his army not against Ireland but against London; and, two years later on the scaffold, one of his followers confessed to Raleigh that they had in fact considered returning suddenly, landing at Milford Haven and marching on London. If this was true,[1] it explains all Raleigh's subsequent conduct. He knew from the beginning the danger of civil war—a state of affairs which, from his youth in France, he had always viewed with the utmost horror and against which he considered no measures too harsh.

When Essex had returned and was still under house arrest, Raleigh wrote to Cecil a letter which has often been construed as an attempt to procure Essex's death. 'I am not wise enough to give you advice; but if you take it for a good counsel to relent against this tyrant, you will repent it when it shall be too late. His malice is fixed and will not evaporate by any of your mild courses. For he will ascribe the alteration to Her Majesty's pusillanimity and not out of any love towards him. The less you make of him, the less he shall be able to harm you and yours. And if Her Majesty's favour fail him, he will again decline to a common person. For after-revenges, fear them not; for your own father was esteemed to be the contriver of Norfolk's ruin, yet his son followeth your father's son and loveth him.'

After giving Cecil several contemporary examples where 'revenge' had been forgotten, he continued: 'I could name you a thousand of those; and therefore after-fears are but prophecies—or rather, conjectures from causes remote. Look to the present and you do wisely. His son shall be the youngest Earl of England but one and, if his father be now kept down, Will Cecil shall be able to keep as many men at his heels as he, and more too. . . .

---

[1] All 'confessions' in this period are suspect: hence the proviso.

But if the father continue, he will be able to break the branches and pull up the tree, root and all. Lose not your advantage; if you do, I read your destiny.'

No one will deny that this letter is, as it has been called, 'calculating, Machiavellian, cold-blooded', though some may reasonably doubt the conclusion of nearly every historian that it is a plea for Essex's execution. It can be more reasonably interpreted as Raleigh's attempt to prevent Cecil using his influence with the Queen to facilitate Essex's return to favour and the cessation of his imprisonment, using the arguments of self-interest which, he knew, would alone appeal to the Secretary.

The advice was not followed. Essex, though he remained banished from the Court, was free again and immediately made Essex House a centre of plotting for rebellion. Though the full truth of his intrigue is not even yet known (we await from some historian a definitive examination of it) it is certain at least that he intended a complete revolution and urged James VI of Scotland to participate in it by insisting that Elizabeth named him as her successor. James did not consider that the time was ripe for so open a move—again, what the reality of negotiations between them was we shall never know, for Essex burnt the correspondence before he was captured—but, when the Scottish King did at last become James I of England, he always referred to Essex as 'my martyr' and maintained an unwavering hatred of Raleigh.

The rebellion, which broke out on Sunday, 8th February 1601, was precipitated by Raleigh's action. For some days councils of war had been held at Essex House, deliberating various plans of action. Rumours were spread abroad that Raleigh and Cecil's brother-in-law, Cobham, intended to murder Essex, so that Essex's proclaimed intention of delivering the Queen from her evil counsellors would appear as a defensive move by a threatened innocent. Had the Court attacked too soon, the populace would have construed it as justifying all Essex's accusations and the consequent rebellion might indeed have become dangerous. But during the Saturday night Raleigh had made a Machiavellian move.

Among Essex's intimates was Raleigh's cousin, Sir Ferdinando Gorges, who held the important post of Governor of Plymouth Fort. As his superior officer, Raleigh ordered him to come and see him at Durham House. Essex could not refuse him permission to go without direct disobedience to lawful authority, but he advised him to meet Raleigh on the neutral ground of the river. To this condition Raleigh agreed, and early on Sunday morning Raleigh kept the rendezvous in a boat alone. Gorges came with two attendants. He had refused to listen to the more violent of Essex's partisans urging him to kill or capture Raleigh, but he was prepared to attempt the latter at least if 'Sir Walter had given me the first occasion by violent deeds or unkind words'.

When the two boats drew alongside, Raleigh merely warned Gorges that a warrant had been issued for his arrest and that he must return immediately to his post at Plymouth if he did not want to find himself in the Fleet prison.

'Tush, Sir Walter,' said Gorges, 'this is not a time to talk of going to the Fleet; get you back to Court, and that with speed, for my Lord of Essex hath put himself into a strong guard at Essex House and you are like to have a bloody day of it.'

Raleigh asked what they intended to do.

'There are two thousand gentlemen', said Gorges, 'who have resolved this day to live or die free men.'

Raleigh answered that he did not see what they could do against the Queen's authority.

'It is the abuse of the Queen's authority by you and others', retorted Gorges, 'that makes so many honest men desire a reformation thereof.'

Raleigh suggested that everyone had to invent an excuse for his actions but besought Gorges to remember his own duty and allegiance.

During this discussion one of Essex's followers on the bank had taken four shots at Raleigh with a musket, each of which had missed him; but now Gorges noticed a boat putting off from Essex Stairs with four musketeers aboard. Suddenly his relationship to Raleigh asserted itself. He shoved his cousin's boat away, bidding him to make haste to escape. So they parted, Raleigh rowing back to Whitehall, Gorges returning to Essex House.

As a sequel four Court officials came to Essex House later that morning and demanded entrance in the name of the Queen. Essex first making them prisoners, led a band of his followers, about three hundred strong, along the Strand and into the City, crying that there was a plot on his life and that England was sold to Spain by the Queen's evil counsellors. But the City did not rise and by the evening Essex and his followers were in prison.

A week later they were brought to trial. Essex pleaded Not Guilty and added: 'I call God to witness, before whom I hope shortly to appear that I bear a true heart to Her Majesty and the country and have done nothing but that which the law of nature commanded me to do in my own defence and which any reasonable man would have done in the like case.' When Raleigh took the oath before giving testimony of his conversation with Gorges, Essex called out: 'What booteth it to swear the fox?' and suggested that a folio would be more appropriate than a small Bible. When Cecil, whose loyalty Essex had impugned, burst into a defence of his innocence, Essex said: 'Ah! Mr. Secretary, I thank God for my humiliation that you, in the ruff of all your bravery, have come hither to make your oration against me this day.' The triumvirate was finally dissolved.

Yet when he came to the scaffold—on 25th February 1601—Essex admitted that Raleigh was a true servant to Queen and State and, in his last moments, asked for him. But Raleigh was not by the block. Though he had at first as Captain of the Guard taken up his position there, the murmuring of spectators, who interpreted the action as a gloating over a rival's death, had caused him to withdraw to the armoury, from the window of which he watched the final act. When it was over, men noticed that his face was bitter with gloom.

Years later, he wrote down for posterity why Essex had died. He and the Queen and Essex were the only three who knew. As Captain of the Guard, he had had to listen, years ago, to Essex hurling insults at him. As Captain of the Guard again, he had heard Essex, at the end, hurl an unpardonable insult at the Queen. 'The late Earl of Essex', he wrote, 'told Queen Elizabeth that her conditions were as crooked as her carcase; but it cost him his head, which his insurrection had not cost him but for that speech.'

CHAPTER TWENTY-ONE

THE SUCCESSION

The two years between the death of Essex and the death of Elizabeth were utilized by Cecil to consolidate his own position and prepare the way for Raleigh's downfall. The Scottish envoys whom James had sent to discuss matters with Essex did not arrive in London until after the Earl's death. They were received by Cecil—secretly, of course, since the Queen would have considered such an action high treason—and assured that he would now undertake to secure the King's succession to the English throne. The enemy, he explained, was Raleigh. In the secret diplomatic correspondence which followed between James and Cecil, the careful blackening of Raleigh continued. And at home the gradual undermining took other forms.

Cecil managed to detach from Raleigh his cousin and friend, Sir George Carew, who was getting tired of being left to cope with the Irish troubles. After a fire at Durham House (which broke out while Raleigh was attending to his official duties in Jersey) Cecil refused Lady Raleigh's request to secure them more than a leasehold interest so that the repair might be worth their expense; on the contrary, as Cecil wanted to get the house taken from the Raleighs, he found the fire and the lack of repairs an excuse for suggesting that they were unsatisfactory tenants.

Above all, Cecil made every effort (through his unrivalled service of spies and *agents provocateurs*) to dissociate himself in men's minds from the death of Essex—who had received 'an unofficial canonization without parallel before or since'—and to lay all the blame on Raleigh. In this he succeeded so well that, by 1603, a gossip was writing: 'Cecil doth bear no love to Raleigh, as you well understand, in the matter of Essex.'

More importantly, Cecil blocked every move to make Raleigh a Privy Councillor, since the post would have given him not only the power to urge his own policies in person but also to defend himself against the Cecilian insinuations at the Council Board. After Essex's fall, there were rumours that he was to be created Earl of Pembroke and, at last and certainly, to become Privy Councillor. Cecil saw that the one was prevented absolutely and that the other was to be made dependent on Raleigh's relinquishing the Captaincy of the Guard—which he knew he would not do.

On the surface, however, all was friendliness. While officially deploring Raleigh's privateering expeditions (for James of Scotland wished to be known as the 'Peacemaker') Cecil invested in them: 'I will be contented to be half-victualler and the rest may be borne between my Lord Cobham and you. . . . But now, Sir, that you know all these particulars, I pray you as much as may be, conceal our adventure, or at the least my name above any other.' He assured his brother-in-law, Cobham and Raleigh 'both in one letter' that his wish is 'to do you both service with all I have and my life to boot'. His son, Will, still visited Sherborne to benefit by the Raleighs' care and kindness.

THE SUCCESSION

One episode at this time reveals both natures. At the beginning of the negotiations for the succession, James, who wished to secure the goodwill of all parties in England, entrusted to his kinsman, the Duke of Lennox, the task of sounding Raleigh. Raleigh, refusing the overture, replied that he was 'over-deeply engaged and obliged to his own mistress to seek favour anywhere else that he should either divert his eye or diminish his sole respect for his own sovereign'. Raleigh told Cecil of this answer, to which Cecil replied: 'You did well and as I myself would have made answer if the like offer had been made to me.'

Raleigh then asked Cecil to tell the Queen of it. The Secretary, terrified that if the subject were raised at all his own machinations would be revealed, 'dissuaded him by many reasons' the last of which was calculated to appeal particularly to the Raleighan temperament—that to make a report of his loyalty 'would be thought a motive to pick a thank'.

This incident has been taken to show that Raleigh was 'after all these years a child in statecraft'; but a truer judgment would be that it shows the extent to which he trusted an apparent friend. Personal treachery was something he never understood.

During these two years, apart from his absences in Jersey and Cornwall, and an excursion into France with Cobham, he divided his time between Sherborne and London. He was still used to entertain visiting celebrities. The Constable of France, whom he took 'to Westminster to see the Monuments' as well as to the Bear Garden, set him a new and unsuspected problem in clothes. He discovered that the French, disdaining the somewhat *nouveau riche* sartorial exuberance of the English Court, wore 'all

black and no kind of bravery at all', and he had hurriedly
to have made 'a black teffeta suit to be in and leave all my
other suits', so that he could be hospitably attired to conduct the French to the Queen at Basing.

Another of his London activities at this period was his
foundation of the most famous of all literary clubs at the
Mermaid Tavern. Its name lives in later literature, but its
atmosphere has been best described by one of its fre-
quenters, the poet-dramatist Francis Beaumont:

> *What things have we seen*
> *Done at the Mermaid! heard words that have been*
> *So nimble and so full of subtle flame,*
> *As if that everyone from whence they came*
> *Had meant to put his whole wit in a jest,*
> *And had resolved to live a fool the rest*
> *Of his dull life.*

In its after-fame the memory of its founder has tended to
be forgotten. Men ask, rather: Was Shakespeare there?
But its spirit was the spirit of Raleigh, as its very name, to
its contemporaries, would recall a traveller's tale.

When at last the Queen died, on 24th March 1603,
Raleigh was in the West and still so unaware of the truth
of the succession arrangements that he is said, when he
arrived in London, to have proposed a republic: 'Let us
keep the staff in our hands and set up a commonwealth
and not remain subject to a needy, beggarly nation.' But,
seeing no escape from the Cecilian *fait accompli*, he set out
to pay his respects to the new King as he made his leisurely progress into England. Cecil saw to it that a Proclamation was issued, aimed specifically at Raleigh, forbidding persons holding public offices to approach the

King before he reached London. Raleigh, who wanted
official sanction for some legal matters in Cornwall, ignored it.

The new King received him with a pun. 'Raleigh!
Raleigh! true enough, for I think very rawly of thee,
mon!' According to another story, which, if not true, is
like those of Raleigh's first meeting with Queen Elizabeth in character, James boasted that, had he wished, he
could have won England by force.

Raleigh replied: 'Would God it had been put to the
trial.'

'Why?' asked James.

'Because your Majesty would then have known your
friends from your foes.'

But about this particular enmity there was never any
doubt. Raleigh set the seal on it at this first interview
(which took place at Beddington Park, where James was
the guest of Lady Raleigh's uncle) by presenting the
'Peace-maker' with his new pamphlet: *A Discourse touching a war with Spain and of the Protecting of the Netherlands.*
He was dismissed from the Captaincy of the Guard; and
given less than a month's notice to leave Durham House.
'I do not know but that the poorest artificer in London
hath a quarter's warning given him by his landlord,' he
commented bitterly. 'To remove my family and stuff in
14 days after is such a severe expulsion as hath not been
offered to any man before this day . . . the course taken
with me is both contrary to honour, to custom and to
civility.'

Worse was to come. Six weeks later—it was some time
between the 12th and 16th of July—he was at Windsor,
waiting to attend the King at a hunt, when Cecil came up

to him 'as from the King' and informed him he was forbidden to go but instead was ordered to appear before the Privy Council to answer certain questions. They concerned a suspected plot to kidnap the King and some letters of Cobham's. Raleigh said he knew nothing about either. He was dismissed, but he was confined to his own house under arrest.

CHAPTER TWENTY-TWO

RALEIGH IS ACCUSED

The accusations framed against Raleigh—and 'framed' may be understood in its modern sense —concerned two supposed plots which marked the opening of James's English reign. They are usually known as the 'Bye' (or 'Surprising') Plot and the 'Main Plot'. The avowed purpose of the first was to kidnap the King and persuade him to grant toleration to Catholics; that of the second the putting of Arabella Stuart on the throne in her cousin James's place. This would ensure a cessation of religious persecution and an alliance with Spain, and the project was to be forwarded by payments from Spain to 'disaffected persons' of whom Raleigh was said to be one.

Raleigh was so obviously innocent of any participation in the kidnapping affair that it may be dismissed immediately. How much he knew of the second remains a mystery. The prime mover in it was his friend, Lord Cobham, and as everybody in the Government, from the King downwards, knew that Cobham was in touch with the Count of Arenberg, Ambassador from the Spanish Netherlands, concerning peace between England and Spain, Raleigh obviously knew that such a negotiation was in being. But whether, in the first place, Cobham had indulged in the treasonable suggestion of forwarding Spain's interests by supplanting James by Arabella and whether, in the second place, Raleigh knew anything about it if he had, are questions which cannot be answered. All that can be said with certainty is that Raleigh, of all people in the world, was never likely to forward the interests of Spain. As he scornfully said at his trial: 'I was not such a madman as to make myself in this time a Robin Hood, a Wat Tyler or a Jack Cade. I knew also the state of Spain; his weakness and poorness and humbleness at this time. I knew that he was discouraged and dishonoured. I knew that six times we had repulsed his forces, thrice in Ireland, thrice at sea—once upon our coast and twice upon his own. Thrice had I served against him myself at sea, wherein for my country's sake I had expended of my own property £4,000. I knew that where beforetime he was wont to have forty great sails at the least in his ports, now he hath not past six or seven; and for sending towards his Indies he was driven to hire strange vessels. . . . I knew that of five and twenty millions he had from his Indies, he had scarce any left.' Was it likely that Raleigh who had so fought against Spain in her greatness should now conspire with her in her weakness? This is the final and unanswerable argument for his innocence, which is untouched by speculations as to how much he knew or did not know of the dreams of that amusing, self-important busybody, Lord Cobham.

When Raleigh was first questioned by the Privy Council, he denied all knowledge of conversations between Cobham and the Netherlands Ambassador; but as soon as he was alone he realized that this diplomatic denial of a fact which every official knew was a foolish action which could be twisted to his disadvantage. He therefore immediately wrote a letter to Cecil qualifying his denial. He had, he said, noticed that Cobham occasionally went to call on La Renzi, one of Arenberg's agents, so that it was possible that conversations were proceeding. This was all Cecil needed. He showed the letter to the unstable Cobham who, assuming that Raleigh had betrayed him, burst out into a wild tirade against him, and exclaimed: 'O traitor! O villain! I will now tell all the truth,' and made a counter-accusation against Raleigh as being the instigator of the scheme. Raleigh was lodged in the Tower.

To understand the sequel it is necessary to jettison any modern ideas of English justice (or, indeed, the sentimentalization of the Elizabethan age usually found in history books) and to think of the time in terms of modern totalitarian government. For this provides the nearest parallel to what may be called the Cecilian system. The rule of Elizabeth (and still more of James, at least in his earlier years) depended on a highly organized reign of terror, in which the forger and the torturer, the spy, the informer and the *agent provocateur* played essential and important parts. Forgery was brought to such perfection that no 'confession' of the time can be claimed as indubitably genuine. One of the unequalled ruffians of history, Topcliffe, was permitted a private torture chamber in which to break the minds and bodies of those inimical to the Government. *Agents provocateurs* sowed in simple minds suggestions of 'plots', which the Government, after nursing them for a time, 'discovered' and used to inflame public opinion against selected sections of the community. As it is impossible to assert the genuineness of a 'voluntary confession', so it is dangerous to assume that any 'plot' against Elizabeth or James was what it seemed to be.

The methods by which men whom the Government

wished to dispose of were brought to trial were only equalled by the manner in which the trials were conducted. Every 'third degree' trick having been used to extort evidence against the prisoner, the prisoner was not permitted to know what that evidence was until he heard it in court. He was allowed no counsel to defend him. He had no chance of cross-examining witnesses. His judges were his political opponents and the verdict of 'Guilty' was a foregone conclusion.

The purpose of such trials was what we should now call propaganda. To the people justice must seem to be done against enemies of the State. That is one reason why 'voluntary confessions' were so prolific; why torture was applied in private and, except in certain cases, such as the Gunpowder Plot, denied in public; why a body of Commissioners, which often included simple and honourable men, sat with the judges, who understood the reality of the proceedings.

The officials who, in the later years of Elizabeth and the early years of James, administered the system were perfectly suited to it. The Lord Chief Justice of England, Popham, began life as a highwayman (he still joined cutpurse bands when he was a barrister), but prudently 'decided to join the safe side of roguery' and eventually died 'with the largest fortune ever amassed by a member of the English bar', the result of a bribery which never benefited his victims. Coke, the Attorney-General (who also made a fortune little inferior to Popham's), was notorious for falsifying evidence if he found that, even after the care with which it was prepared, it was inconvenient, and for his habit of bullying and insulting witnesses in a manner which equalled, if it did not exceed, that of the later Judge

Jeffreys. Waad, a creature of Cecil's, who has been rightly called 'one of the meanest men of a time exceptionally rich in such', was in charge of preliminary investigations, as became so accomplished a spy-master, with his private entourage of torturers and forgers. Cecil, whose master hand controlled them all, we already know.

Raleigh knew them too. He had no illusions about his position. When he was arrested, he wrote to his old comrades-in-arms, Lord Howard and Lord Thomas Howard, who were among those chosen as Commissioners, asking not to be sent 'to the cruelty of the law of England' and when he knew that the trial was to go forward, he made an attempt at suicide so that, dying before sentence, he might save his estates for his wife and son. But he wounded himself only slightly and recovered both life and courage. His enemies accused him of conspiring to deprive the King of his sovereignty by making Arabella Stuart Queen; of having, with Cobham, promised to act in the interests of Spain once her succession was secured; of having lent Cobham a treasonable book against the King's title to the throne; of having been promised 8,000 crowns of the Spanish money and other similar charges; though 'only part of this farrago of nonsense was seriously pressed when it came to his trial'. The absurdity of the accusations was, however, irrelevant. The argument had no connection with justice.

It was another kind of fight, and Raleigh would outface his powerful enemies as he outfaced the London mobs who, for the memory of Essex, tried to lynch him as he was taken through the London streets on his way to Winchester, where, because of an outbreak of the plague in the capital, his trial was to be held.

CHAPTER TWENTY-THREE

THE TRIAL

The trial opened on November 17th—the first November 17th for forty-five years which had not been celebrated as 'Accession Day'. The symbolism of it, as the last great Elizabethan stood at bay, was inescapable, and spectators must have heard an overtone, to which readers of the trial are deaf, when Raleigh the poet suddenly described Elizabeth in her old age as 'a Lady whom Time had surprised'. And as the trial proceeded, it was the Raleigh of the cool head and quick tongue which had first fascinated the dead Queen, who took the centre of the stage.

Coke opened the attack by recalling the Bye Plot and the Main Plot and enlarging on Cobham's treason. Raleigh remarked: 'I do not hear yet that you have spoken one word against me; here is no treason of mine done. If my Lord Cobham be a traitor, what is that to me?'

Coke replied that behind Cobham's feeble brain was 'Raleigh's devilish and machiavellian policy'.

Coke: All that he did was by thy instigation, thou viper; for I 'thou' thee, thou traitor.

Raleigh: It becometh not a man of quality and virtue to call me so; but I take comfort in it. It is all you *can* do.

Coke: Have I angered you?

Raleigh: I am in no case to be angry.

Coke did his best to make Raleigh lose his temper. He called him a 'damnable atheist'. He told him he was a monster with 'an English face but a Spanish heart'. He screamed at him—

Coke: Thou art the most vile and execrable traitor that ever lived.

Raleigh: You speak indiscreetly, barbarously and uncivilly.

Coke: I want words sufficient to express thy viperous treason.

Raleigh: I think you want words indeed, for you have spoken one thing half a dozen times.

Coke: Thou art an odious fellow. Thy name is hateful to all the realm of England for thy pride.

Raleigh: It will go near to prove a measuring cast between you and me, Mr. Attorney.

There was, of course, no evidence whatever against Raleigh except Cobham's confession. Raleigh pointed out that according to the law of England, two witnesses were needed to convict a man of treason. He was told that in this case, as Cobham himself was also on trial, his witness counted as it was the unanimous decision of a jury of twelve men.

Raleigh produced a letter which Cobham had written him, clearing him of the treason. 'To clear my conscience, satisfy the world and free myself from the cry of your blood,' Cobham had written, 'I protest upon my soul, and before God and His angels, I never had any conference with you in any treason; nor was ever moved by you to the things I heretofore accused you of. And, for anything I know, you are as innocent and as clear from any treasons against the King as is any subject living.' Raleigh was told that this letter was invalid, since it had been written under pressure. Raleigh had assured him, while they were both in the Tower, that since two witnesses were required, they were safe. The intermediary who carried the letters was Raleigh's faithful friend, Kemys, whose testimony was thus the more damning.

Coke: Cobham saith that Kemys came to him with a letter, torn; and did wish him not to be dismayed, for one witness could not hurt him.

Raleigh: This poor man hath been close prisoner these eighteen weeks. He was offered the rack to make him confess. I never sent any such message by him. I only did write to Cobham to tell him what I had done with Mr. Attorney, I having of his at that time the great pearl and a diamond.

Howard: No circumstance moveth me more than this! Kemys was never at the rack. The King gave charge that no rigour should be used.

The Other Commissioners: We protest, before God, there was no such matter to our knowledge.

Raleigh: Was not the Keeper of the Rack sent for; and he threatened with it?

Waad: When Mr. Solicitor and myself came to examine Kemys, we told him he deserved the rack, but did not threaten him with it.

The Other Commissioners: It was more than we knew.

Raleigh then asked to be allowed to confront Cobham there in court. The Statutes of England guaranteed at least that the accuser should thus repeat his accusation. But this, to the prosecution, would have been fatal.

Popham: The Statutes you speak of were found to be inconvenient and were taken away by another law.

Raleigh: I know not how you conceive the Law.

Popham: Nay, we do not conceive the Law. We *know* the Law.

On the matter of the treasonable book which Raleigh was said to have lent to Cobham, there was momentary consternation in court.

Raleigh: Here is a book supposed to be treasonable. I never read it nor commended it nor urged it. I had it out of a Councillor's library long since.

Coke: What Councillor?

Raleigh: My Lord Treasurer Burleigh.

This brought Cecil, irritated and embarrassed, to his feet:

Cecil: You may remember that, after the death of my father, you desired of having some cosmographical maps and books of that kind, concerning discoveries of the Indies and Western parts. I allowed you a search; but if, under colour of this, you extended the liberty to other things I meant not, you abused my trust. To find a book of that kind there was not hard. For no book that touched the State, nay, scarce a libel that in the Queen's time had been spread against the State, but amongst those papers it might have been found—he being a Councillor of State—and so, perhaps, may be yet found with me. Therefore let it not seem strange to any that such a book was found there. But you did wrong, Sir Walter Raleigh, to take it thence—

Raleigh: There was no purpose in taking that book. But amongst other books and maps it seems it was cast in. Upon sorting of the papers afterwards, it came to my hand. It was a manuscript, written upon by my Lord Treasurer 'This book had I of Robert Snagge'. The scope of the book is to justify the late Queen's proceedings against the Queen of Scots. But I marvel it should now be urged as a matter so treasonable in me to have such books, when it is well known that there came out nothing in those times but I had them and might as freely have them as another. How my Lord Cobham came by this book I know not, but I remember that it lay upon my board at a time when he was with me.

In spite of this contretemps, 'even Cecil seems to have had some qualms during the trial he had engineered'. He wanted the ruin of Raleigh, but—for the sake of all that had been—not his death. At one point he even reproved Coke.

Cecil: Be not so impatient, good Master Attorney. Give him leave to speak.

Coke: If I may not be patiently heard, you will encourage traitors and discourage us. I am the King's sworn servant, and must speak. If he be guilty, he is an odious traitor; if not, deliver him.

Thereupon Coke sat down in a rage and had to be coaxed for some time before he would continue his oration.

And, at the end of the trial, Cecil tried to prevent Raleigh from falling into a trap which the prosecution had prepared for him. Believing himself, in fact, cleared by Cobham's letter to him, Raleigh said he would stand or die by what Cobham said. Cecil warned: 'Then call to God, Sir Walter, and prepare yourself!' For Cecil knew that Cobham had, under Government pressure, written another letter, retracting his retractation and asserting 'in duty to my Sovereign and in discharge of my conscience' that Raleigh had tried to get him to procure a pension of £1,500 from Spain in return for regular information of 'what was intended against Spain'. On hearing this last and unforeseen lie 'Sir Walter Raleigh was much amazed', though 'by and by he seemed to gather his spirits again'. But he was beaten and he knew it.

Nevertheless, he too played his last card. He produced from his pocket an even later letter from Cobham and handed it to Cecil to read, as he could identify the hand-writing: 'Seeing myself so near my end, for the discharge of my own conscience and freeing myself from your blood, which else will cry vengeance against me, I protest upon my salvation I never practised with Spain by your procurement—God so comfort me in this my affliction as you are a true subject for anything I know. So God have mercy on my soul, as I know no treason by you.'

'Now I wonder how many souls this man hath!' re-marked Raleigh. 'He damns one in this letter and another in that.'

For a moment there was confusion in court. Then the Lord Chief Justice came to the rescue by pointing out that Cobham's letter to the King was a voluntary one, whereas his letter to Raleigh was obviously the result of pressure. Judicial paradox could hardly go further. The jury, how-ever, understood what was expected of them, and after a retirement of fifteen minutes, found Raleigh guilty of high treason. Even Coke was surprised. He was resting in the garden after his labours when a messenger brought the verdict to him. 'Surely thou art mistaken,' he said, 'for I myself accused him but of misprision of treason!'

It was left to Popham as Lord Chief Justice to do what further damage he could to the prisoner in his summing-up. He emphasized Raleigh's reputed atheism and his friendship with Harriot: 'Let not any devil Harriot, nor any such doctor, persuade you there is no eternity in Heaven. If you think thus, you shall find eternity in Hell fire.' Then, after remarking with a pious shudder: 'I never saw the like trial and hope I shall never see the like again,' he pronounced the terrible sentence of death by hanging, disembowelling, mutilation and quartering.

Others also thought they had not seen a like trial. One of the judges, Gawdy, confessed that 'never before had the justice of England been so depraved and injured as in this trial'. And in the country, Raleigh's rehabilitation was sweeping and complete. Almost overnight, as the reports of the trial spread, Raleigh from being the best-hated man in England became the most revered. Even Essex was forgotten. 'Never was a man', wrote one of the letter-writers of the day, 'so hated and so popular in so short a time.' And the report of one of the King's official observers may stand as an epitome for all: 'Whereas when I saw Sir Walter Raleigh first, I would have gone a hundred miles to see him hanged, I would, ere we parted, have gone a thousand to save his life.'

CHAPTER TWENTY-FOUR

AWAITING EXECUTION

The execution was appointed to take place at Winchester on December 13th. In prison, awaiting the end, Raleigh suffered the inevitable reaction from his effort at the trial. To Cecil, to the Commissioners, to the King he wrote letters in the most abject terms begging for his life. But once more his courage reasserted itself, and in his farewell letter to his wife he urged: 'Get those letters, if it is possible, which I writ to the Lords, wherein I sued for my life. God knoweth it was for you and yours I desired it, but it is true that I disdain myself for begging for it. And know, dear wife, that your son is the child of a true man who, in his own respect, despises Death and all his misshapen and ugly forms.'

It is this letter, from which one or two quotations have already been made, which gives most truly the picture of Raleigh during these days: 'You shall receive, dear wife, my last words in these my last lines. My love I send you that you may keep it when I am dead; and my counsel that you may remember it when I am no more. I would not, with my last Will, present you with sorrows, dear Bess. Let them go to the grave with me and be buried in the dust. And, seeing that it is not the will of God that ever I shall see you in this life, bear my destruction gently and with a heart like yourself.

'First I send you all the thanks my heart can conceive or my pen express for your many troubles and cares taken for me, which—though they have not taken effect as you wished—yet my debt is to you never the less. But pay it I never shall in this world.

'Secondly, I beseech you, for the love you bare me living, that you do not hide yourself many days, but by your travail seek to help your miserable fortunes, and the right of your poor child. Your mourning cannot avail me that am but dust. . . .

'And I trust my blood will quench their malice that desire my slaughter, and that they will not also seek to kill you and yours with extreme poverty. To what friend to direct thee, I know not, for all mine have left me in the true time of trial; and I plainly perceive that my death was determined from the first day. Most sorry I am (as God knoweth) that, being thus surprised with death, I can leave you no better estate. . . . If you can live free from want, care for no more, for the rest is but vanity. Love God, and begin betimes to repose yourself on Him; therein shall you find true and lasting riches and endless comfort. For the rest, when you have travailed and wearied your thoughts on all sorts of worldly cogitations, you shall sit down by Sorrow in the end. Teach your son also to love and fear God while he is young, that the fear of God may grow up in him. Then will God be a husband unto you and a father unto him; a husband and a father which can never be taken from you. Remember your poor child for his father's sake that chose and loved you in his happiest times. . . .

'I cannot write much. God knows how hardly I stole this time, when all sleep. And it is time to separate my thoughts from the world. Beg my dead body, which living was denied you; and lay it at Sherborne, if the land continue, or in Exeter church by my father and mother. I can write no more. Time and Death call me away.

'The everlasting, infinite, powerful and inscrutable God, that Almighty God that is goodness itself, mercy itself, the true life and light, keep you and yours and have mercy on me, and teach me to forgive my persecutors and false accusers; and send us to meet in His glorious kingdom. My true wife, farewell! Bless my poor boy; pray for me. My true God hold you both in His arms.'

That was for her alone. To the world he gave a different farewell—a poem which mirrored his life. It recalled, by its symbol of the poor pilgrim, the device he had used in his poems to Cynthia and the world that that implied. The pilgrims who had preceded him had Elizabethan names all Europe knew. The jewelled country evoked memories of Guiana and a journey on which thirst had been a nightmare reality. The closing scene at Winchester dominated it, but not so direly that he could forgo a pun about 'angels' or refuse to contemplate the outcome with a savage realism far from courtly conceits. The company at the Mermaid would surely have applauded *The Passionate Man's Pilgrimage*.

> *Give me my scallop-shell of Quiet,*
> *My staff of Faith to walk upon,*
> *My scrip of Joy, immortal diet,*
> *My bottle of Salvation,*
> *My gown of Glory, Hope's true gage,*
> *And thus I'll take my pilgrimage.*

AWAITING EXECUTION

Blood must be my body's balmer,
No other balm will there be given,
Whilst my soul like a white palmer
Travels to the land of Heaven,
Where spring the nectar fountains;
And there I'll kiss
The bowl of bliss,
And drink my everlasting fill
On every milken hill.
My soul will be a-dry before,
But after it will thirst no more.

And by the happy blissful way
More peaceful pilgrims I shall see,
That have shook off their gowns of clay
And go apparrelled fresh like me.
I'll bring them first
To slak their thirst,
And then to taste those nectar suckets
At the clear wells
Where sweetness dwells,
Drawn up by saints in crystal buckets.

And when our bottles and all we
Are filled with immortality,
Then the holy paths we'll travel
Strewed with rubies thick as gravel,
Ceilings of diamonds, sapphire floors,
High walls of coral and pearl bowers.

AWAITING EXECUTION

From thence to Heaven's bribeless hall
Where no corrupted voices brawl,
No conscience molten into gold,
No forged accusers bought and sold,
No cause deferred, nor vain-spent journey,
For there Christ is the King's Attorney,
Who pleads for all without degrees,
And he hath angels but no fees.

When the grand twelve million jury
Of our sins and direful fury
'Gainst our souls black verdicts give,
Christ pleads His death, and then we live.
Be Thou my speaker, taintless pleaser,
Unblotted lawyer, true proceeder;
Thou mov'st salvation e'en for alms,
Not with a bribed lawyer's palms.

And this is my eternal plea
To Him that made Heaven, earth and sea:
Seeing my flesh must die so soon,
And want a head to dine next noon,
Just at the stroke when my veins start and spread,
Set on my soul an everlasting head.
Then am I ready, like a palmer fit,
To tread those blest paths which before I writ.

But the stroke was not, after all, to fall just yet. At the
last moment he was reprieved and sent not to the scaffold
at Winchester but to imprisonment for life in the Tower
of London.

CHAPTER TWENTY-FIVE

THE TOWER

Raleigh remained a prisoner in the Tower for over twelve years—that is to say, for a period as long as that between his first coming to Court and the granting of the patent for Guiana. For him, the circumstances of that little confined world must have been as varied as those of the great one, and month by month there was the expectancy of release. But, from the outside, we have lost the pattern of it. To us the endless succession of hope-disappointed days is no more than a period of Raleigh's life—perhaps the finest—when his mind went adventuring though his body could not. To it belong his great prose writings including the *History of the World*, his scientific experiments, his naval treatises, his friendship with Henry Prince of Wales who gave promise, had he lived, of being one of the greatest of English kings, the very masterpiece of Raleigh's making.

To the fact of imprisonment were added the circumstances of it. From his quarters in the Bloody Tower he wrote to Cecil (now promoted to the peerage), whose true nature he was at last realizing: 'Whatsoever your Lordship hath conceived, I cannot think myself to have been either an enemy or such a viper but that this great downfall of mine, this shame, loss and sorrow, may seem to your Lordship's heart and soul a sufficient punishment and revenge. And if there be nothing of so many years' love and familiarity to lay in the other scale, O my God! how have my thoughts betrayed me in your Lordship's nature, compassion and piety. For to die in perpetual prison I did not think your Lordship could have wished to your strongest and most malicious enemies. . . . I have presumed at this time to remember your Lordship of my miserable estate—daily in danger of death by the palsy, nightly by suffocation by wasted and obstructed lungs; and now the plague being come at the next door unto me, only the narrow passage of the way between. My poor child having lain this 14 days next to a woman with a running plague sore and but a paper wall between, and whose child is also this Thursday dead of the plague. . . . My most humble desire is to be removed elsewhere, even to what place which God's goodness, and Charity, shall move your Lordship's heart. . . .'

With the letter he enclosed an inventory of his property showing that his income now amounted to no more than £295 a year—which just paid for his keep at the Tower. He was a pauper dependent on his wife's private money. Both she and their son came to live with him in the early days of his imprisonment, but she eventually took a little house on Tower Hill where their second son, Carew, was born in 1605. She visited her husband daily, insisting on driving in to the Tower in her coach, to the exasperation of the Governor, who eventually took steps to prevent such display.

This Governor was the mean spy-master Waad who had been one of Raleigh's judges and was appointed to the Tower in 1605 in time to deal with the Gunpowder conspirators. But for the first year of his imprisonment

Raleigh had the benefit of a governor, Sir George Harvey, who had become one of his admirers and who did
all he could to mitigate the imprisonment which Cecil
refused to alter. Harvey allowed Raleigh to use his private
garden and even to build there a little hut in which he
could conduct his chemical experiments.

Waad, after a week in office, wrote to Cecil that 'Sir
Walter Raleigh hath converted a little hen-house in the
garden into a still, where he doth spend his time all the
day in his distillations. I desire not to remove him, though
I want, by that means the garden. . . . If a brick wall were
built it would be more safe and convenient.' The wall was
built, and by 1606 when the atmosphere of the rooms in
the Bloody Tower had done their work, and Raleigh had
suffered a slight stroke on his left side, he was allowed to
build a small room by his laboratory and live in that
seclusion.

This spot became famous throughout Europe—for, as
the Government were uneasily recognizing, wherever Sir
Walter Raleigh sat, even as an imprisoned pauper, was
head of the table. There was a recrudescence of the early
legends of alchemy and necromancy, given more colour
by the fact that 'the School of Night' was in being again
in the Tower. In 1606 the 'Wizard Earl', Northumberland, was imprisoned there for alleged complicity in the
Gunpowder Plot and Harriot was now of his household,
while the faithful Kemys was sharing Raleigh's imprisonment.

But more immediately impressive were the practical
results of Raleigh's experiments. His 'Great Cordial or
Elixir', a 'Balsam of Guiana', was reputed to cure all
diseases except those which resulted from poison. It did,

in fact—or so she believed—save the life of the Queen, who remained one of his firmest friends. It did for a moment (though it was given too late) revive Prince Henry on his death-bed. It was sought by visiting nota-bilities and a little of it procured by the wife of the French

Part of Raleigh's notes, made in the Tower, for the preparation of crystalline mercury sublimate (crystalline mercuric chloride).

Ambassador. The formula remains Raleigh's secret, though some have thought it to have been quinine. In addition to the Elixir, which gave him a new international reputation, Raleigh in his converted hen-house discovered a method of obtaining fresh water from salt, which was not rediscovered for two centuries, and developed a pro-cess of tobacco-curing.

Such activities hardly recommended him to King James, who disliked his wife only a little less than he abominated tobacco—against which he wrote a *Counterblast*, pointing out that 'it makes a kitchen of the inward parts of men, soiling and infecting them with an unctuous and oily kind of soot' and that smoking is 'a custom loathsome to the eye, hateful to the nose, harmful to the brain, dangerous to the lungs, and in the black stinking fume thereof nearest resembling the horrible Stygian smoke of the pit that is bottomless'.

It is impossible to escape the conclusion that the King, who prided himself on being a writer, a poet and a philosopher, was irritated by his prisoner's pre-eminence even here—he ordered the suppression of Raleigh's *History of the World* when it appeared—and that, behind the puerile assumptions of the *Counterblast* there was an intended antagonism to the discoverer of tobacco.

The most severe blow the King and Cecil dealt Raleigh in prison was the taking from him of Sherborne. In 1602, in the uncertainty of the days before Elizabeth's death, he had had the estate conveyed to his son, reserving a life interest to himself and £200 a year to his wife as long as she lived. The clerk who had drawn the deed up, however, had omitted ten words—'shall and will henceforth stand and be thereof seized'—and when Coke and Popham were consulted on the matter, they found that this omission invalidated the transference. This news which came in 1605 just after the birth of Raleigh's second son, caused Lady Raleigh, for the first and only time, to reproach her husband. Raleigh wrote to Cecil that 'she hath already brought her eldest son in one hand and her sucking child in another, crying out of her and their destruction, charging me with unnatural negligence, and that, having provided for mine own life, I am without sense and compassion of theirs'.

Cecil did nothing, so Lady Raleigh sought an audience with the King and begged him to overlook a lawyer's clerk's negligence. Face to face with her, James gave in, assured her that Sherborne should remain the Raleigh home and instructed Cecil to have a new grant legally drawn. Cecil (whether with or without the King's secret connivance cannot be said with certainty) carefully omitted to do so.

In 1607 the King chose the most despicable of his long succession of favourites, a handsome young boor named Kerr, whom he made successively Viscount Rochester and Earl of Somerset. One of the first necessities was to find him a country estate. Cecil suggested Sherborne, which delighted both the King and Kerr, and legal proceedings were instituted against the Raleighs. Once more Lady Raleigh visited Court. James ignored her. She fell on her knees 'beseeching God Almighty to look upon the justness of her cause and punish those who had so wrongfully exposed her and her poor children to ruin and beggary'. James merely muttered: 'I mun have the land. I mun have it for Kerr,' and early in 1608 the judges decided that he could. The scandal, however, had to be softened by an appearance of Royal generosity. The King would allow Lady Raleigh £5,000 in commutation of her life interest.

Raleigh, in desperation wrote direct to Kerr: 'Seeing your day is but now in the dawn and mine come to the evening ... I beseech you not to begin your first buildings on the ruins of the innocent and that their griefs and sorrows do not attend your first plantation'—a wasted plea to the unscrupulous minion, though the King did make one further concession. The £5,000 was raised to £8,000, with a pension of £400 a year to Lady Raleigh.

It was Henry, Prince of Wales, now a boy of fifteen but far older than his years, who upset James's plans. He went in a rage to his father, told him that Sherborne was a place of too great beauty and strength to be alienated from the Crown and demanded it for himself. James gave way and compensated Kerr for the loss by a gift of £25,000. Everyone understood what this move meant. The Prince would hold it for Raleigh and return it to him as soon as he was released.

The friendship between the Prince and Raleigh was one of the mitigating circumstances of the imprisonment. On his accession the prisoner would be 'the power behind the throne', and the Prince's scornful remark: 'None but my father would keep such a bird in a cage,' was generally known and appreciated. As it was, Raleigh, through Henry, could still intervene in politics, and when proposals were made for the Prince's marriage, it was Raleigh who wrote a *Discourse touching Marriage between Prince Henry of England and a Daughter of Savoy*. Through Henry, Raleigh could still put into practice his unrivalled naval knowledge. In the October of 1608 the keel of the *Prince Royal* was laid—the first English naval three-decker, built to Raleigh's specifications—and such writings as a *Letter to Prince Henry on the Model of a Ship* and *Observations concerning the Royal Navy and Sea-Service* made his experience accessible to those who could benefit by it.

Through the Prince's intervention matters had, indeed, progressed so far that James had consented to release Raleigh at the Christmas festivities of 1612. But in November Henry died, and all was black again.

Cecil also died that year. There were many epitaphs on him, among them—so it was reputed—one from Raleigh. It is unprintable, as most of them were. Of the remainder, the simplest and most apt was:

Here lies Robin Crookback; unjustly reckoned
A Richard the Third, he was Judas the Second.

CHAPTER TWENTY-SIX

THE HISTORY OF THE WORLD

Any fool', it has been said, 'can make history, but only a wise man can write it.' Raleigh had had his share in the one; now he would wed his experience with his learning and attempt something never before done—the writing of the history of the world. The work was undertaken for Prince Henry and was dedicated to him. The Prince's request for a fuller treatment of the story of the Greeks and Romans held up the first publication (it was entered in the Stationers' Register in 1611) and his death put an end to the composition of it. The book as we have it ends with the Roman conquest of Greece in the second Macedonian War and fills over a thousand large pages of Raleigh's collected works, but later volumes were planned—already, in fact, as the author put it, 'hewn out'. But Henry's death and Raleigh's complete breakdown in health, resulting in a second stroke, meant an end of the writing.

This very great book, incomplete as it is, is Raleigh's masterpiece. In spite of the King's attempt to suppress it, it had an immediate success when it appeared in 1614; it went through three editions in 1617 alone, and another eight before the end of the century; it influenced men as different as Milton and Montrose; Hampden studied it deeply and Oliver Cromwell recommended it to his son;

it was the constant companion of the Princess Elizabeth, Henry's sister, Rupert's mother. If, in later centuries, it fell into disfavour, that was partly because, either through lack of faith in God or excess of faith in 'scientific method', men came to repudiate Raleigh's underlying philosophy of history. He saw it—as the Bible sees it—as the dealings of God with men. Individuals, not 'movements', interest him: the inscrutable will of God not a discoverable 'pattern of history' is the constant: 'God, whom the wisest men acknowledge to be a power ineffable and virtue infinite: a light by abundant clarity invisible: an understanding which only itself can comprehend; an essence eternal and spiritual, of absolute pureness and simplicity: was and is pleased to make Himself known by the work of the world'—thus it opens. To find 'causes' in history may be easy but unprofitable. The simple understand the 'how' of things as easily as the learned, but neither knows the 'why': 'the cheeswife knoweth as well as the philosopher that sour runnet doth coagulate her milk into a curd.' What is interesting is the spectacle of individual destinies, for Nature delights in apparent variety. 'Change of fortune in the great theatre is but as change of garments in the less, for when on the one or the other every man wears but his own skin the players are all alike.' And this relationship of the Many and the One is mirrored from the lowest to the highest. In a perfect simile—inspired by his memory of the Orinoco delta—he sums it up: 'Certainly, as all the rivers in the world, though they have divers risings and divers runnings, though they sometimes hide themselves for awhile underground and seem to be lost in the sea-like lakes, do at last find and fall into the great ocean: so after all the searches that human

157

capacity hath and after all philosophical contemplation and curiosity, in the necessity of this infinite Power all the reason of man ends and dissolves itself.'

Only at death do men understand reality. 'It is therefore Death alone that can suddenly make man to know himself. He tells the proud and insolent that they are but abjects, and humbles them at the instant, makes them cry, complain and repent, yea, even to hate their fore-passed happiness. He takes the account of the rich and proves him a baggar, a naked baggar, which hath interest in nothing but the gravel that fills his mouth. He holds a glass before the eyes of the most beautiful and makes them see therein their deformity and rottenness: and they acknowledge it.' This passage leads to the famous apostrophe to Death, which has been rightly called the most perfect prose in the English language: 'O eloquent, just and mighty Death! Whom none could advise, thou hast persuaded; what none hath dared, thou hast done; and whom all the world hath flattered, thou only hast cast out of the world and despised; thou hast drawn together all the far-stretched greatness, all the pride, cruelty and ambition of man and covered it over with these two narrow words, *Hic Jacet.*'

With such a philosophy as the foundation of the structure of his history, Raleigh drew on his experience of statecraft to elucidate the past and, with some cynicism, to enunciate the truth, self-evident but continually shirked, that modern and contemporary history is, in any age, impossible: 'I know it will be said by many that I might have been more pleasing if I had written the story of mine own times, having been permitted to draw water as near the well-head as another. To this I answer that whosoever in writing a modern history shall follow Truth too near the heels, it may haply strike out his teeth.' And the vignettes he drew, in passing, in the preface more than justified him. It was his reference to Henry VIII—'if all the pictures and patterns of merciless princes were lost in the world, they might all again be painted to the life out of the story of this king'—that caused James to order the suppression of the book, on the ground that the author was 'too saucy in censuring princes'.

It is possible, also, that James understood that even ancient history can so be written as to have a modern application and objected to the reminder that Jehoram's slaughter took place in Naboth's vineyard—'that field which, purchased with the blood of the rightful owner, was watered with blood of the unjust possessor' brought Jezreel surprisingly near Sherborne. And a topical but uncomplimentary allusion might be detected in the reference to the Queen Semiramis and her successor: 'Her son, having changed nature and condition with his mother, proved no less feminine than she was masculine.'

The philosophy of the history was Raleigh's and the style and the experience which revivified the past, but for the actual collection of material and the checking and collating of facts, he had naturally to rely on many helpers. Harriot and Kemys and Ben Jonson (who, as one of the Mermaid circle, had become his friend and was now tutor to his son, Walter) were his great helpers, and there were others who formed the circle about the imprisoned Northumberland who were still free in the larger world. But, making all allowance for the necessary co-operation implied by an encyclopaedic effort, the conception and the achievement of the *History* were Raleigh's alone and, even to-day, when so many great writers have turned to history, it is still true of the book that it is lit with 'a personal illumination we can find in hardly any historian'.

Raleigh and his elder son, Wat

A portrait by Giesharz, once at Wickham Court, Kent, but destroyed
in the war by enemy action

CHAPTER TWENTY-SEVEN

WAT

Young Walter Raleigh—'Wat'—was the same age as Prince Henry. Both boys were born in 1594; both, in looks, resembled their mothers rather than their fathers; and both suffered that adolescent reaction against their fathers which is not uncommon in eldest sons. In Henry's case this reaction was intense, justified and, since he was heir to the throne, of considerable consequence. In Wat's case it was, perhaps, comprehensible—for it must have been more difficult to grow up under the shadow of Raleigh's personal greatness and public ruin than under James's weakness and royalty, and whereas Henry would have found it difficult not to be better than James, Wat must have been early aware that his place in history could never be other than that of the great Raleigh's son. But the tensions between Raleigh and Wat had no wider interest than that of adding to Raleigh's sorrow, for he loved the boy intensely and saw in his unbiddable wildness the ghost of his own youth.

Wat was only nine at the time of Raleigh's trial and to have had at that age to change the magic grounds and the great house at Sherborne for a lodging with his father in the Tower or with his mother in her little house on Tower Hill would go far to explain a mute and puzzled resentment, which his father's obvious delight in the company of Prince Henry would do nothing to allay. Yet even at Sherborne Wat had showed a wildness that had caused Raleigh to write a sonnet to him, which must surely be unique as verses from a father to his small son:

> *Three things there be that prosper up apace*
> *And flourish, whilst they grow asunder far;*
> *But on a day they meet all in one place,*
> *And when they meet they one another mar.*
>
> *And they be these; the Wood, the Weed, the Wag.*
> *The Wood is that which makes the gallows-tree.*
> *The Weed is that which strings the hangman's bag.*
> *The Wag, my pretty knave, betokeneth thee.*
>
> *Mark well, dear boy, whilst these assemble not,*
> *Green springs the tree, hemp grows, the wag is wild;*
> *But when they meet, it makes the timber rot,*
> *It frets the halter and it chokes the child.*
>
> *Then bless thee, and beware, and let us pray*
> *We part not with thee at this meeting day.*

Perhaps the most characteristic story of Wat concerns an episode which probably took place during the years in prison. Raleigh was invited to dinner with 'some great person'—it may have been the Earl of Northumberland —and was asked to bring his son with him. Raleigh told Wat frankly that he was 'such a quarrelsome, affronting' so-and-so that he was 'ashamed to have such a bear' in his company. Wat promised to behave himself and, at first, it seemed that he would keep his word, for 'he sat next to his father and was very demure at least half dinner time'. Then, carefully choosing his time and speaking with slow deliberation, he made an exceedingly coarse remark. 'Sir Walter, being strangely surprised and put out of countenance at so great a table, gives his son a damned blow over the face. His son, rude as he was, would not strike his father, but strikes over the face the gentleman that sat next to him and said: "Box about; 'twill come to my father anon." '

Raleigh's paternity was only too obvious and, indeed, he himself seems to have realized how like Wat was to himself when young, without his wife's constant reminders of it. In his *Advice to his Son*, written in prison, he makes his own weaknesses a text to warn Wat. His extravagant splendour was still a legend when he wrote solemnly: 'Exceed not in the humour of rags and bravery, for these will soon wear out the fashion; but money in thy purse will ever be in fashion; and no man is esteemed for gay garments but by fools and women.'

Raleigh saw to it, too, that Wat had the best education he could provide—in the early days such tutors as Harriot, Kemys and Raleigh himself; then Oxford, and in 1613 (the year after Henry's death) a year in France with Ben Jonson. We have no evidence of Wat's scholastic attainments, but the episode of his getting his new tutor dead drunk (no difficult feat with Ben Jonson) and then having him trundled through the streets of Paris 'on a car', stopping and exhibiting him at each street corner, suggests that War remained very much his usual self.

The young man was abroad again in the spring of 1615, this time in the Low Countries, where he had fled after wounding one of the Lord Treasurer's household. Being a Raleigh, his reason for the journey was not safety but a desire to finish the fight. He brought his opponent with him and although the English Ambassador did his best to pacify them, he had to report that interference 'will, I think, rather defer than prevent this evil, for the difference between them is irreconcilable'.

Wat, however, was shortly to find another outlet for his energies. His father's release was now near at hand and he was to accompany him, as a captain, to Guiana.

CHAPTER TWENTY-EIGHT

RELEASE

Guiana, through all the long years in the Tower, had never been forgotten. Every two years some kind of ship had been sent to keep Raleigh in touch with the Indians there. The burden of his pleas to Cecil and the King was that, if he might go again to Guiana, he could provide enough gold to fill the Exchequer now emptied by the King's wild extravagances. In 1609 one of his friends, Harcourt, had been allowed to attempt to found a colony in the land 'lying between the Rivers of Amazons and Orenoque, not being actually possessed and inhabited by any other Christian Prince or State'. The Indian tribes, however, while welcoming Harcourt, made it plain that they wanted Raleigh.

Yet how, the King asked, could he send a disgraced prisoner on such an errand? Would it not be 'a great levity of state'? To this Raleigh retorted that there might be objections 'if I had desired the trust of any great sum of money, of any great army or any great fleet, or of anything else whereby your Majesty might have received prejudice'. But Raleigh was risking nothing but himself and his reputation. The Crown would be in no way committed.

James and Cecil decided to send, in 1610, not Raleigh but Sir Thomas Roe. In order not to annoy the Spaniards it was given out that the expedition was meant for Virginia, though Roe's secret instructions were to explore the region between the Orinoco and the Amazon. This Roe did with some care, leaving there a small new colony and pointing out how impossible it was to keep peace with the Spaniards who 'use us whose hands are bound with any contumely and treachery'. He also reported that the story of Manoa and El Dorado was nothing but a myth—a circumstance which led to a notable dwindling of interest on the King's part, who was interested only in gold.

But Raleigh himself never gave up hope, even though the King's foreign policy in the next few years altered the whole aspect of the 'Spanish Main'. In 1613 a new Spanish Ambassador, usually known in history by his later title of Count Gondomar, was sent to London with instructions to 'keep the King good' and rapidly, by the force of his character and his psychological acumen, established over James something amounting to a private dictatorship. In 1614 negotiations were actually set on foot for the marriage of Prince Charles (by Henry's death the heir to the throne) with the Infanta of Spain. In 1615 Spain was sure enough of James's subservience, in his desire for peace and an alliance, to order their Governor of Trinidad and Guiana to 'extirpate utterly' the English settlers and traders whom Raleigh and Kemys and Harcourt and Roe had left in those regions. This, needless to say, was as unknown to Raleigh as it was to the country in general. Raleigh did not know either that the new Ambassador hated him above all living Englishmen, partly on patriotic grounds and partly on personal (for his uncle had once been captured by one of Raleigh's privateers).

This new pattern of foreign policy was to give to the rest of Raleigh's life a twist of almost unbearable dramatic irony; but it was another irony—this time in Court affairs—which was to bring about his release and demonstrate a change of circumstance worthy of pride of place in his *History*.

The King had grown tired of that Robert Kerr, Earl of Somerset, to whom he had given Sherborne. He had, in 1614, noticed a new and even better-looking young man, named George Villiers (whom, in the usual way, he eventually made Duke of Buckingham). His interest in Villiers was such that he refused to intervene to rescue Somerset from the danger in which he had become involved by reason of his wife's having poisoned his friend. Both the Earl (who was probably innocent) and the Countess (who was undoubtedly guilty) were made to stand their trial and, after a series of sensational revelations, were found guilty. Once more Raleigh's home was wanted for them, and in 1616 Raleigh's cousin, Carew, could write to Sir Thomas Roe, now Ambassador in India: 'The Earl of Somerset hath the liberty of the Tower, which he useth very sparingly. His wife and he lodge together; he lies in the Bloody Tower, Sir Walter Raleigh's ancient lodging, and she in Sir Walter's new buildings.'

According to one story—which, like others of the Raleigh legend, may or may not be true—Raleigh and Somerset met here for the first and last time as Raleigh was removing his possessions from his 'hen-house'. Raleigh remarked: 'My whole *History* has not the like precedent of a King's chief prisoner purchasing freedom and his bosom-favourite having the halter; but it is in Scripture—Mordecai and Haman.' James, when he heard it, sent back to Raleigh the menacing answer: 'You may die in this deceit'—which, indeed, the King saw to, for in the end it was Raleigh who was killed and Somerset who was pardoned.

Raleigh's reference to his purchase of freedom was his gift of £750 each to two members of the family of Villiers, the new favourite. Everything else had been unavailing—his own innocence, his own promises, the anger of England, the intercessions of Prince Henry and the Queen—so at the end he took the conventional Jacobean way.

His first action on leaving the Tower was to walk all over London to see the changes which had taken place during his imprisonment. This itself was a voyage of discovery, for the new buildings and alterations were extensive. The King, in fact, had the previous year claimed, not altogether without reason: 'As it was said of the first Emperor of Rome that he had found the city of Rome of brick and left it of marble, so We, whom God hath honoured to be the first of Britain, might be able to say in the same proportion, that we had found our City and suburbs of London of sticks and left them of brick, being a material far more durable, safe from fire and beautiful and magnificent.' Smithfield had been paved and Moorfields planted; Aldgate had been 're-edified' and two new hospitals, as well as Hicks's Hall, built; there was the New River and, of particular interest to Raleigh, the New Exchange—Britain's Burse—which Cecil had had built on part of the grounds of Raleigh's own Durham House.

Raleigh was not, of course, allowed at Court. From the actual day of his release, 19th March 1616, to the day,

RELEASE

30th January 1617, when the King 'fully and wholly enlarged him', he was still officially attended by a keeper.
Nor was his liberty even then without conditions. He was
now to do that for which he had so long pestered and
promised—to find gold in Guiana.

CHAPTER TWENTY-NINE

PREPARING TO SAIL

The new expedition was Raleigh's death-trap and everyone but himself and his immediate circle knew it. A friend of Kemys wrote to him:

Raleigh, in this thyself thyself transcends,
When, hourly tasting of a bitter chalice,
Scanning the sad faces of thy friends,
Thou smils't at Fortune's menaces and malice!

Hold thee firm here: cast anchor in this port!
Here art thou safe till Death enfranchise thee.
Here neither harm, nor fears of harm, resort;
Here—though enchained—thou livest in liberty.

He was a man still under sentence of death, for though he had been reprieved the Winchester verdict had never been quashed. His patent was originally prepared in the correct form to 'Our Trusty and Well-Beloved' under the Great Seal (which would, of course, imply a complete pardon), but, in deference to Gondomar's protest against the expedition of 'that old pirate in particular, bred under the English virago, and by her fleshed in Spanish blood and ruin', James erased the 'Trusty and Well-Beloved' and made it under the Privy Seal only. Raleigh was forbidden to enter Spanish territory or to fight the Spaniards. James promised Gondomar that if he dared even look at Spanish property he would send him to be hanged in chains in the Plaza of Madrid. The King then insisted that Raleigh should hand over a complete itinerary of his expedition, as well as a list of his ships and their armament, which 'on the hand and the word of a king', he promised to keep secret. As Raleigh might have guessed had he known James better, this formula was the guarantee of betrayal. James communicated everything to Gondomar, who sent it to Madrid, with the result that the Spaniards were prepared at every point to force a fight.

In short, Raleigh, in undertaking the expedition, was out of date. In his mind he still imagined things the Elizabethan way. Often enough the Queen had openly condemned, for reasons of international politics, raiding expeditions at which she had secretly connived. Once before, royal disfavour had omitted the 'Trusty and Well-Beloved' in one of his patents. But the upshot had not been disastrous. Nor would it be this time. When Francis Bacon (Cecil's cousin who shared his Judas-taint) asked him what he would do if, after all, he did not find the gold-mine, Raleigh answered: 'We will look after the Plate Fleet, to be sure.'

'But then you will be pirates,' warned Bacon.

Raleigh laughed: 'Oh, no! Whoever heard of men being pirates for millions?'

Here, probably, he was right. Had he brought home millions, by whatever means, James, Gondomar notwithstanding, would not have dared to withhold pardon.

It was assumed by many—and those not only in England—that once Raleigh put to sea he would indeed turn pirate. As the expedition was a private one, he had not the right to press men for his service but had to rely on volunteers; and these volunteers were the very dregs of the nation whose personal intentions were certainly piracy. He himself described them as 'the very scum of the world, drunkards, blasphemers and such-like' who 'left their country for their country's good'. No one expected them to return. Men said that if they sunk it would save the King the expense of halters to hang them.

Nevertheless, preparations proceeded. £30,000 was raised in joint stock, chiefly from Devon. Lady Raleigh sold for £2,500 her own estate, while £3,000 of the Sherborne compensation money was added to the fund. The Government gave £175 as a bounty to encourage shipbuilding and the construction of the ships started in the Thames, supervised by Raleigh. His own flagship, of 440 tons, he named the *Destiny*, in which Wat was to sail with him, Captain to his Admiral. There were the *Star* and the *Encounter*, the *Thunder* and the *Flying Joan*—altogether seven ships of war with three pinnaces, carrying about a thousand men. In the March of 1617 they were ready to leave the Thames and make their way to Plymouth, from which, as was proper, the expedition was to sail.

Plymouth itself, 'by general consent', entertained them at public expense and even paid a drummer to call them to the feast. When they finally put out to sea, joined by three other ships outside the harbour, they left in an atmosphere of enthusiasm which even the West, in its unfaltering loyalty to Raleigh, had never exceeded.

But Gondomar had made his preparations too. He wrote immediately to the King of Spain to inform him that the expedition had now set out 'indifferently equipped both as regards men and provisions, but with very good guns and munitions of war', whereupon the King took immediate steps 'to put an end to this enterprise as well as the lives of all who go with Don Gualtero Rauli'.

The King of England also played his part. The Captain of the Guard reported to one of Cecil's old associates who acted as a spy for Spain: 'His Majesty is very disposed and determined against Raleigh and will join with the King of Spain in ruining him, but he wishes this resolution to be kept secret for some little while in order that . . . he may keep an eye on the disposition of some of the people here.'

CHAPTER THIRTY

THE SECOND VOYAGE TO GUIANA

As so often in Raleigh's voyages, the weather at setting out was unpropitious. Twice he was driven back to the English coast, once to Plymouth itself and once to Falmouth. On the third attempt a pinnace sank off the Scilly Islands, and the rest of the little fleet had to put into Kinsale Harbour for refitting. During their ten days' stay in Ireland Raleigh visited his old estate at Lismore as the guest of the new owner, Lord Boyle, to whom he had sold it. Here he indulged once more in a sport he had once loved when Elizabeth was alive—falconry—and when, on 19th August 1617, the expedition once more put out to sea, his host replenished his wasted stores by the gift of a hundred oxen and other eatables, including biscuit; a thirty-two gallon cask of whisky and a liberal supply of beer.

On September 7th they reached Lancerota in the Canary Islands, where they decided to take in water. The Spanish Governor gave them permission, but when they landed they found that the Spaniards had decamped into the interior and had informed the natives that the English were Barbary pirates. They were, under this misapprehension, attacked, and lost fifteen men. Raleigh restrained his men from vengeance and merely sent the Governor a message that, were he not so careful to give no offence to his own king, he would have pulled him and his people out of the town by the ears.

Obedience to the terms of his commission could hardly go further, yet at this point Captain Bailey (who was spying on him for the Government) deserted and returned to England with the news that Raleigh was about to do what general rumour had predicted he would do—turn pirate. James thereupon sent an official message to Gondomar to express 'the great sorrow of all good people at what Raleigh has done'. Gondomar reported triumphantly to his master: 'The King promises he will do whatever we like to remedy and redress . . . so atrocious a wickedness as this', and suggested that a Spanish fleet should immediately be sent to capture Raleigh's expedition (which, because of its size, would be easy enough), to kill all the members of it except Raleigh and his officers, who could be taken to Seville for public execution.

Meanwhile Raleigh, unaware of this new treachery, had sailed on to Gomera, the last port of call in the Canaries. Here his reception was very different, because the Governor's half-English wife was delighted to welcome her famous compatriot. Nor did the courtliness of Raleigh fail her expectation of him. He sent her six pairs of gloves, six fine kerchiefs, an ounce of delicate extract of amber, a great glass of rosewater, 'a very excellent picture of Mary Magdalen' and a cutwork ruff. She in return, as Raleigh entered in his *Journal*, sent 'four great loaves of sugar, a basket of lemons, which I much desired to comfort and refresh our sick men, a basket of oranges, a basket of most delicate grapes, another of pomegranates and figs, which trifles were better welcome to me than 1,000 crowns would have been'. Before sailing, he was also given more fruit, some white bread, 'two dozen fat hens', and allowed all the water he needed. Moreover, the Governor gave him a letter to take back to Gondomar 'witnessing how nobly we had behaved ourselves and how justly we had dealt with the inhabitants of the island'.

The fruit was to save Raleigh's life. The rest of the journey was a tempest-tossed nightmare, made more hideous by an outbreak of fever which claimed forty-two men on the *Destiny* alone. The crossing 'that hath ever been sailed in fourteen days' was 'now hardly performed in forty days'. Raleigh himself caught a chill which turned to fever, and for a whole month could take no solid food. But for the fruit, he wrote to his wife, 'I could not have lived'. And when at last, on November 14th, they sailed safely into the mouth of the Cayenne River, he had a relapse and his life was despaired of.

But once more the indomitable will won. He fought his way back to some sort of health, though he was still too feeble for there to be any possibility of his leading an expedition inland. His recovery was aided by the Indians' welcome. After twenty-two years the great Englishman had returned to them as he had said he would. 'To tell you that I might be King of the Indians were a vanity,' he wrote to Bess, 'but my name hath still lived among them. Here they feed me with fresh meat and all that the country affords; all offer to obey me.' He was carried ashore and put in a tent. Once more in his Earthly Paradise, he found himself 'exceedingly tempted' by those pineapples whose potent juice he remembered, but discretion triumphed and he continued to take only the lemons from Gomera, so carefully eked out and preserved in sand. Only when he was out of danger did he enter in his *Journal*: 'I

Raleigh the Statesman

A portrait of Raleigh in 1598. In the corner hangs a plan of the Cadiz action. He is supporting himself on the walking-stick which he needed because of the lameness resulting from his wound in that fight

began to eat of the pine, which greatly refreshed me, and after that I fed on the pork of the country and of the Armadillios and began to gather a little strength.'

Immediately on landing he sent one ship back to England with news that Guiana was reached. That much at least had been accomplished. But he did not disguise the toll which the crossing had taken or the precariousness of the situation. Gondomar was delighted. The official recital of facts he embellished with any unofficial scandal he could pick up from the returned crew. To the tale of the dreadful voyage, with its deaths, disease and shortage of food, he added: 'All those who have come hither agree that nothing but entire failure can be expected from Raleigh's voyage, and they think that those who remain with him will either be lost or, if they are able to get out, will turn pirates.' Even those who wished Raleigh well were disheartened, and one letter of the time records that Raleigh's news 'come charged with misfortunes and tears and his wife is in great affliction'.

Raleigh, indeed, had by now no illusions about his danger. Part of the King's treachery he knew, though the full revelation was still to come. 'We are yet', he told his wife, 'strong enough I hope to perform what we have undertaken, if the diligent care at London to make our strength known to the Spanish king by his ambassadors have not taught the Spanish king to fortify all the entrances against us. Howsoever, we must make the adventure.' But even more dangerous than the fortifications they might encounter on the way up the Orinoco to the mine was the possibility that the new 'armada' which, rumour had it, was being prepared would come down to block the mouth of the river and hold them like rats in a trap. To guard against this situation, Raleigh, even had he been strong enough to lead the expedition, could not have done so. He must stay in Trinidad to keep open their line of retreat. The men refused to go in search of the mine at all unless their Admiral gave them his word that, whatever happened, they would find him at the river's mouth when they returned.

'You shall find me at Puncto Gallo (Trinidad), dead or alive,' said Raleigh. 'And if you find not my ships there, you shall find their ashes.'

And with this assurance from the one man they trusted, five vessels of shallow draught, carrying 400 men, set off down the Orinoco once more. In command was, inevitably, the faithful Kemys, who had travelled that way before. With him were Raleigh's nephew, George, and Wat.

CHAPTER THIRTY-ONE

AWAITING NEWS

Kemys's instructions were to make his way to the mine, to bring back enough ore to convince the English Government that gold was indeed to be found there, to refrain from attacking the Spaniards, though if attacked to repel them, and, should the mine itself be guarded, to—in Raleigh's words—'be well advised how you land, for I know (a few gentlemen excepted) what a scum of men you have, and I would not for the world receive a blow from the Spaniards to the dishonour of our nation'. The party set off on 10th December 1617, and arrived in sight of their goal three weeks later.

About the subsequent events there has been from that day to this unending controversy. What was Raleigh's real intention? Did Kemys exceed instructions? Were there *two* mines, one at Mount Aio just before the Spanish settlement of San Thomé, and one near the Caroni River where Raleigh himself had turned back on the first voyage, just beyond it? Had the site of the settlement itself been moved since Kemys saw it during his expedition in 1596? (It had not been there at all on Raleigh's own visit of 1595.) Were Raleigh and Kemys counting on a rising of the Indians against the Spaniards? Various historians have elaborated various theories, yet, for all their brilliance in reconstruction, the full truth is never likely to be known.

What is certain is that the English did not trespass on Spanish territory and that they did not fight till they were attacked. Unfortunately, however, Raleigh's reputation had to wait 380 years before it was vindicated and it was only in 1928 that Mr. Milton Waldman, in his biography of Raleigh, first drew attention to the fact of this vindication in the proceedings (between 1896 and 1899) of the Venezuelan Boundary Commission. As these findings supersede all the earlier evidence, it is worth quoting Mr. Waldman's epitome.

'The conclusions are', he says, 'that between 1596 and 1720 the Spaniards had not extended their possessions beyond the immediate confines of San Thomé; that from 1613 and 1618 the Spaniards "were definitely excluded to the eastward of the Orinoco" (in other words, the right bank where Kemys landed was unoccupied territory); that the constant trading by the English, and especially the Dutch, systematically and not on sufferance, precludes the idea of Spanish political control. . . . Raleigh's own Government has held, in short, that he had actually done only what his commission permitted him to do, penetrated into the "parts of America . . . possessed by heathen and savage people". The mine lay outside the "confines" of San Thomé; hence it was his right to seek it out, and repel the efforts of anyone to hinder him in his legitimate occupation.'

Thus in the events of the next few weeks and their tragic outcome neither Raleigh nor Kemys, whatever other mistakes might be made, can be held guilty of contravening King James's almost impossible instructions.

AWAITING NEWS

After Kemys's departure, Raleigh sailed to the place of rendezvous in Trinidad. Though he tried to establish friendly contact with the Spaniards on the island, they attacked him and killed two of his people by musketry fire. This was on 19th January 1618. Raleigh made no counter-attack, but continued to explore the remoter parts of the island for medicinal plants and rare herbs, in the intervals of cruising along the coasts, watching for the possible Spanish fleet.

The first news he had of the party on the Orinoco was gossip from some Indians passing him in a canoe. It was rumoured that the English had stormed a Spanish town and that two captains had been killed in the attack. Immediately Raleigh started to question every native he came across. Every day he sent out a new party in search of news. But it was not until February 14th that a messenger arrived bearing a letter from Kemys, written five weeks earlier. The Admiral now knew the worst. The Spanish settlement of San Thomé had been taken and Wat Raleigh was dead.

CHAPTER THIRTY-TWO

SAN THOMÉ

Kemys and his party, on their two-hundred-mile journey up the Orinoco, had been perpetually harassed by Spanish fire from the banks, and when eventually they landed on 1st January 1618, not far from the settlement of San Thomé, an ambuscade was ready for them. While the English were debating the best course to take, a Spanish patrol fell on them at one in the morning, with shouts of '*Perros Engleses*' (English dogs). Taken completely by surprise, 'the common sort, as weak sort as ever followed valiant leaders, were so amazed as, had not the captains and some other valiant gentlemen made a head and encouraged the rest, they had all been broken and cut to pieces'.

It was Wat Raleigh, his father's son, indeed, who rallied them. Crying: 'Come on, my hearts! This is the mine you must expect. They that look for any other are fools!' he ran forward, practically alone. Heartened by this example, the men followed and found themselves at the town 'almost before themselves knew of it'. But Wat fell, mortally wounded. His last words—'with constant vigour of mind being in the hands of death'—were: 'Go on! Lord have mercy on me and prosper your enterprise.'

At the attack the Spaniards fled, except for the Governor (a relative of Gondomar) and two captains, who were killed. The total casualties were ten—five English, five Spanish—and the English held San Thomé. The dead were buried, Wat Raleigh in a place of honour before the high altar in the little church. And in his letter to his father, Kemys ascribed to him all the credit: 'Had not his extraordinary valour and forwardness led them on, when some began to pause and recoil shamefully, this action had neither been attempted as it was, nor performed as it is, with this surviving honour.'

Nevertheless, quite apart from its later political repercussions, the attack on San Thomé was a tactical error. The Spaniards now concentrated their forces on an island at the junction of the Orinoco and the Caroni and spread others hiding in the forests, so that it was the English who were the hunted. When Kemys took a party up the Orinoco intending to turn down the Caroni towards the mine, Spanish fire killed or wounded all but one of the occupants of one of the two launches and he was forced to go back to San Thomé. Eventually it was George Raleigh who took the initiative and led an expedition up the Orinoco for another two or three hundred miles. But he returned empty-handed to the garrison of San Thomé, who were now hungry, terrified and besieged by snipers. Kemys had actually hung out white flags, inviting a parley, but the Spaniards preferred to continue their successful jungle warfare. There was now no alternative to returning. Having held San Thomé for four weeks and a day, they burnt it to the ground and started the grim journey back.

Raleigh received Kemys as kindly as he could. They dined and supped together. But, as full realization of the catastrophe dawned on Raleigh, he could not refrain from recriminations. When Kemys explained the four reasons which led him to abandon the search for the mine—the death of Wat; the weakness of the English and the impossibility of victualling them while they were working; the foolishness of showing the Spaniards where the mine was; and the fact that Raleigh himself was too weak to go there, and that, as he was still unpardoned, all their lives were in danger at home—Raleigh burst out: 'You have undone me and wounded my credit with the King past recovery; and seeing my son is lost, I should not have cared if you had lost a hundred more in opening the mine, so that my credit had been saved.'

In mounting fury and misery, he added that Kemys could answer for himself to the King why, being so near, he had shrunk back from opening the mine.

Kemys, seeing argument was useless, said he would go to his own hut and 'wait on him presently and give him better satisfaction'. A moment or two after he had left him, Raleigh heard a pistol shot. He shouted to Kemys to know what it was. Kemys called out that he had been firing his pistol off to clean it. When, after an interval, Kemys did not return, Raleigh went on search of him. He found him dead with a knife through his heart. The pistol shot had merely glanced off his rib. The second time he left nothing to chance.

There was one further depth for Raleigh to plumb. Among the things Kemys had brought back from San Thomé was the list of ships and men and the itinerary which Raleigh had given to King James—not merely a copy, but the original list in Raleigh's own hand. He now knew the extent of the treachery and the certainty of the trap—and that he must soon follow his son and his friend.

SAN THOMÉ

Next day he wrote to the Secretary of State an official account of his failure. He revealed his broken heart—'my son was slain, with whom to say truth all respect of the world hath taken end in me'—and asked the Secretary to comfort his wife and to give her a copy of his report. He made it clear that he knew the reality of things at last: 'For it pleased His Majesty to value us so little as to command me, on my allegiance, to set down under my hand the country, and the very river by which I was to enter it; to set down the number of my men and burden of my ships; with what ordnance every ship carried; which, being made known to the Spanish Ambassador, and by him, in post, sent to the King of Spain, a despatch was made by him, and his letters sent from Madrid before my departure out of the Thames.'

He explained why the mine was not worked. 'Lastly, to make an apology for not working the mine—although I know not (his Majesty excepted) whom I am to satisfy so much as myself, having lost my son and my estate in the enterprise—yet it is true that the Spaniards took more care to defend the passages leading unto it than they did their town, which (say the King's instructions) they might easily do.'

Next day he wrote to his wife: 'I was loth to write, because I knew not how to comfort you: and, God knows, I never knew what sorrow meant till now. All I can say to you is that you must obey the will and providence of God: and remember that the Queen's Majesty bare the loss of Prince Henry with a magnanimous heart, and the Lady Harrington of her only son. Comfort your heart (dearest Bess), I shall sorrow for us both. I shall sorrow the less, because I have not long to sorrow because not long to live. I refer you to Mr. Secretary Winwood's letter, who will give you a copy of it if you will send for it. Therein you shall know what hath passed. I have written but that letter, for my brains are broken, and it is a torment for me to write, and especially of misery. . . . You shall hear from me if I live, from the Newfoundland where I mean to make clean my ships and revictual. . . . The Lord bless and comfort you, that you may bear patiently the death of your valiant son.'

That was all that he meant to write, but he changed his mind and added a postscript, four times as long as the letter, telling her the whole story: 'I protest before the majesty of God that as Sir Francis Drake and Sir John Hawkins died heartbroken when they failed of their enterprise, I could willingly do the like, did I not contend against sorrow for your sake in hope to provide somewhat for you and to comfort and relieve you,' he assured her. 'If I live to return, resolve yourself that it is the care for you that hath strengthened my heart.'

Then, having despatched his testaments, he decided that old, weak and broken as he was, he would lead a second expedition to the mine and either bring back the gold or leave his body beside his son's.

CHAPTER THIRTY-THREE

GONDOMAR VICTORIOUS

Raleigh's letters did not reach London till 23rd May 1618, but long before that Gondomar had had his way with James. In March the King had renewed his promise that the 'pirate' should be sent for execution in Spain, and in April the Ambassador received congratulation from his own master. 'Your Excellency's account of the conference you had with the King about Raleigh's affair pleased our people here so much that they found it almost too sweet,' wrote Philip's secretary. 'It really seemed too much that Raleigh should be sent hither.' On May 13th, by way of Madrid, the news of San Thomé reached England. Gondomar burst in on James in spite of the message that he was occupied to say 'one word only'. He roared it three times: 'Pirate! Pirate! Pirate!' and left the King terrified.

After Raleigh's letters had been delivered the bearer of them was questioned. He added fuel to the flame by informing James that the only thing of value which had been brought from San Thomé was tobacco. Early in June the King issued a Proclamation, expressing affection for 'our dear brother, the King of Spain', and detestation for the 'scandalous and enormous outrages' of Raleigh who had 'maliciously broken and infringed the peace'. Privately he assured Gondomar that 'Raleigh's friends and all England shall not save him from the gallows', and reiterated his promise that, after a short but necessary judicial examination, Raleigh should be handed over to die publicly in Spain.

Though the Privy Council, venal as the majority was, protested against this extraordinary procedure, James wrote a letter for Gondomar—who was returning on leave to Spain early in July—to take to his master, promising that, after an examination in England, 'which cannot altogether be avoided', Raleigh should be sent to Spain, 'with ten or a dozen of the worst' of his men, in the *Destiny* itself, unless Philip himself decided otherwise.

This was the situation, unparalleled in all the annals of England, to which, on June 21st—the twenty-second anniversary of the day when Raleigh had sailed with trumpets blowing between the Spanish ships at Cadiz— the *Destiny* returned alone into Plymouth Harbour.

Raleigh's plan to lead a new expedition in search of the mine had been overruled by a Council of War. He had then decided to visit Virginia, which he longed to see, and prepare a new venture for the Orinoco the following spring. He had been opposed in this by two of his captains, who suggested as an alternative that they should turn unofficial pirates in the Elizabethan way and capture Spanish ships at sea. When he refused, they left him and turned pirates on their own account.

He had now, beside the *Destiny*, only three ships left. He dared not, in the end, put in at Virginia, for he had discovered that if he did more than a hundred of his crew, including some of the gentlemen, intended to stay there and join the colonists. So he set off across the Atlantic once more to find what awaited him at home. The men, who had no mind for it, mutinied and only allowed him to sail provided he promised to land them in Ireland. From here they refused to follow him further and stayed safely in Kinsale Harbour. So it was that, on that June day, the *Destiny* sailed into Plymouth alone. But it was a greater gesture than the trumpets at Cadiz.

No one expected the return. Raleigh's cousin, Carew, who, as a member of the Privy Council, knew the truth of the situation, sent a message to Plymouth: 'Get you gone!' Both the French and the Dutch would have welcomed Raleigh's service. A letter-writer summed up the general feeling: 'The world wonders extremely that so great a wise man as Sir Walter Raleigh would return to cast himself upon so inevitable a rock as I fear he will.' Lady Raleigh met him and told him of the King's Proclamation against him. But he refused to fly. As Lord Admiral he ordered his relative, Sir Lewis Stukeley (Grenville's nephew), who was Vice-Admiral of Devon, to arrest him. But Stukeley, as yet undecided what to do, did nothing, and Raleigh was left at least a fortnight's grace in which he could have escaped if he had wished. Instead, resisting his wife's entreaties to find safety for himself, he set down a quiet recital of the facts of the expedition and sent it to Carew to present to the Privy Council.

In it, he pointed out that he had been warned by his men that 'if I returned home poor I should be despised, and I answered that even if I were a beggar I would not be a robber, or do anything base, nor would I abuse the confidence and commission of the King. Before doing this I would choose, not poverty alone, but death itself. I am well aware that with my ship (than which in the world there is no better) I could have enriched myself by £100,000 in the space of three months and could have collected a company which would have impeded the traffic of Europe. But those who have told the King I feigned the mine and really intended to turn pirate are now mistaken in their malice, for, after failing in the discovery of the mine (by the fault of another), and having lost my estate and my son and being without pardon for myself or security for my life, I have held it all as nought and offer myself to His Majesty to do with me as he will without making any terms.'

As for the taking of San Thomé, 'it was impossible to avoid, because when the English were landed at night to ensure Kemys's passage, the Spaniards attacked them, killing several and wounding many. Our companies then pursued them, and found themselves inside the town before they knew it. It was at the entrance of the town that my son was killed, and when the men saw him dead they became so enraged that, if the King of Spain himself had been there in person, they would have shown him but little respect.'

In the last section of the letter he went to the root of the charges against him in a contemptuous attack on James's policy: 'And, my Lord, that Guiana can be Spanish territory can never be acknowledged, for I myself took possession of it for the Queen of England by virtue of a cession of all the native chiefs of the country. His Majesty knows this to be true, as is proved by the concession granted by him under the Great Seal of England to Harcourt.'

James, when he received it from Carew, gave a copy of the letter to Gondomar, so that Spain might know what

Raleigh's defence would be. Then he sent a peremptory message to Sir Lewis Stukeley: 'We command you upon your allegiance that, all delays set apart, you do safely and speedily bring hither the person of Sir Walter Raleigh to answer before us such matters as shall be objected against him.'

CHAPTER THIRTY-FOUR

BETRAYAL

The case against Raleigh, despite all the King could say or do, was extremely weak and time was not on the Government's side. Feeling in the country, at every level, was rising. If Raleigh's friends were hopelessly outnumbered on the Council, they were in a majority in the kingdom. But they were leaderless, unorganized and unaware of what was happening. Parliament, except for two abortive months in 1614, had not been in session for eight years and was not to be summoned for another three. James's rule was, in fact, an effective dictatorship, functioning through Favourites; and the Favourite of the moment, Buckingham, was, if possible, even more pro-Spanish and anti-Raleigh than the King himself. Yet there was always a chance of a revolt against this corrupt rule (there was, in fact, an armed revolution in little more than twenty years) and Raleigh, with Londoners' feelings rising against Gondomar, could easily have been the centre of it. The one necessity of the Government was, therefore, to discredit Raleigh and make him, in some way, convict himself. To this end, they surrounded him with spies and *agents provocateurs*.

The chief of them was Sir Lewis Stukeley himself, who for his activities in the matter became known as Sir Judas Stukeley—a nickname which has persisted through his-

Lady Raleigh in her widowhood with her younger son, Carew

This portrait, which has never hitherto been reproduced, is now in the possession of Mrs. Hilda D'Arcy Sykes, who has kindly allowed its reproduction here

tory. As Raleigh's cousin, Stukeley was the less likely to
be suspected by him, and his protestations of loyalty to
Raleigh and sympathy with him were, of course, un-
bounded.

As a useful accomplice he used a French doctor named
Manourie, who had actually brought the warrant of
arrest. Manourie won Raleigh's confidence by skilfully
talking chemistry and was able to note certain 'treasonable' remarks, such as Raleigh's outburst as the party rode
through Sherborne: 'All this was mine and it was taken
from me unjustly.' But it seems that Raleigh's charm
worked on his charmer, for Manourie became his accomplice in a piece of high comedy which temporarily dis-
comfited Stukeley.

Raleigh wanted time to prepare a full defence, his
Apology for the Voyage to Guiana, and also a chance to
present it to the King himself, who was at Salisbury on
the summer Progress. The necessary quiet and delay could
be gained only by illness; and though Raleigh was far
from well, his symptoms were not such as would justify
a break in the journey. He therefore asked Manourie to
make him up some preparations which would produce
the appearance of some dangerous disease. As soon as the
party reached Salisbury, Raleigh pretended to have a
spell of dizziness, struck his head against a post and asked
Stukeley, who was helping him to his bedroom, to send
Manourie to him. Manourie came and gave him the desired concoction. Raleigh was violently sick, managed to
have convulsions and by the additional treatment of an
ointment smeared on the skin, came out in great blotches.
Stukeley, fearing the plague, was reduced to a state of
terror, and rushed over to Winchester to see Lancelot

Andrewes, the bishop, who was also a Privy Councillor, to ask what he should do. Andrewes sent three doctors back to Salisbury who, after a long consultation, signed a bulletin that Raleigh's condition was extremely serious and that he must on no account be moved, though they privately admitted that they were completely at a loss to know what the illness was.

Having gained his objective, Raleigh was 'very jocund and merry with Manourie', who managed to smuggle in 'a leg of mutton and three loaves' from the White Hart Inn to the now ravenously hungry patient. Thus refreshed, Raleigh wrote feverishly through the night his *Apology*. 'It is', as Edward Thompson described it, 'superb in rushing indignation and strength, from the very first sentences which take the field like a man with sword unsheathed and brandished.'

'If the ill success of this enterprise of mine had been without example', Raleigh began, 'I should have needed a large discourse and many arguments for my justification. But if the vain attempts of the greatest princes of Europe . . . have miscarried, then it is not so strange that myself, being but a private man, and drawing after me the chains and fetters wherewith I had been thirteen years tied in the Tower, being unpardoned and in disgrace with my Sovereign King, have by other men's errors failed in the attempt I undertook.'

And, after he had told again the tale we know, he ended by attacking his real antagonist: 'But in truth the Spanish Ambassador hath complained against me to no other end than to prevent any complaint against the Spaniards. . . . My men were invaded and slain before any violence was offered to any of the Spaniards; and I hope the Ambassador does not esteem us for so wretched and miserable a people as to offer our throats to their swords without any manner of resistance.'

But Raleigh was not allowed to present the *Apology* to James. The King may well have found his mere presence in Salisbury alarming and refused to see him. Instead, he angrily ordered Stukeley to continue immediately the journey to London.

They reached the capital on August 7th and Raleigh was allowed to stay at Lady Raleigh's house in Broad Street. Here, for the last time, his friends gathered round him and, in spite of the danger, there was an atmosphere of hope once more. Two days later the French Ambassador called on him and offered to put a French ship at his disposal to take him safely across the Channel to an honourable welcome in France. Raleigh refused, not, this time, the chance of escape—for at last he had decided to make a bid for it—but the means. He would gladly go to France, but not as a passenger in a French vessel.

One of his faithful captains, King, had, with Lady Raleigh, gone ahead of the rest from Salisbury and arranged for one of Raleigh's old seamen to take him across the Channel. Unfortunately the plan had been communicated to another servant, Cottrell, who was secretly in Stukeley's service and who, as soon as the details were completed, gave Stukeley all the necessary information. Stukeley thereupon became more affectionate than ever towards his cousin, protested that, should he think of making his escape, he would go with him, wherever it was, and so was taken completely into the unsuspecting Raleigh's confidence.

That same night, August 9th, Raleigh, with King,

Stukeley and some servants, set out down the Thames in two wherries to the ship waiting at Gravesend to bear him to safety. They were followed by a larger boat, in which, by Stukeley's arrangement, was a party under the command of Sir William St. John, ready to act at the right moment.

The moment came when, having lost the tide, Raleigh landed at Greenwich. Stukeley embraced Raleigh affectionately and kept him in conversation while the pursuers landed silently. As soon as escape was impossible, 'Sir Judas' officially arrested Raleigh and King.

Raleigh said: 'Sir Lewis, these actions will not turn out to your credit.' Then he turned to King and asked him to pretend, for his own safety, that he was Stukeley's accomplice. King refused. At Traitor's Gate, Raleigh made a last effort to comfort him: 'You need be in fear of no danger. It is I only that am the mark shot at.'

'I was forced to take my leave of him,' King wrote afterwards. 'I left him to His tuition, with Whom, I doubt not, his soul resteth.'

CHAPTER THIRTY-FIVE

THE TOWER ONCE MORE

Raleigh's old enemy, Waad, was no longer Lieutenant of the Tower. He had been dismissed for embezzlement and was living in wealthy retirement in his mansion at Belsize Park. The new Lieutenant, Sir Allen Apsley, had been with Raleigh in the Cadiz action and showed the imprisoned hero what kindness he could. When Raleigh was stripped of his personal possessions by Stukeley—they included such diverse odds and ends as a Guiana idol of gold and copper; a jacinth seal, set in gold, with a Neptune cut in it and a piece of Guiana ore attached; a naval officer's whistle of gold set with diamonds; a diamond ring given him by Queen Elizabeth; maps of Guiana and the Orinoco—he refused to surrender to him the miniature he always carried, but was content to leave it in Apsley's keeping.

Yet in spite of his goodwill, Apsley was powerless to protect him from Wilson, one of Cecil's old spies, whom the Government set to watch him and, by the usual pretence of friendship and solicitude, to try to trap him into an appearance of treason. But Raleigh, at last and too late, was on his guard. Wilson could get nothing from him and had to be content with reporting to James such trivialities as: 'The things he seems to make most recking of are his chemical stuffs, amongst which there are so many spirits of things that I think there is none wanting that ever I heard of, unless it be the spirit of God.'

Raleigh himself wrote to the King one last blazing letter: 'If in my journey outward bound I had some of my men murdered at the Islands and spared to take revenge; if I did discharge some Spanish barques taken, without spoil; if I forbare all parts of the Spanish Indies, wherein I might have taken twenty of their towns on the sea-coast, and did only follow the enterprise I undertook for Guiana —where, without any direction from me, a Spanish village was burnt, which was newly set up within three miles of the mine—by Your Majesty's favour I find no reason why the Spanish Ambassador should complain of me.

'If it were lawful for the Spanish to murder 26 Englishmen, tying them back to back and then to cut their throats, when they had traded with them a whole month and came to them on land without so much as one sword amongst them all—and that it may not be lawful for Your Majesty's subjects, being forced by them, to repel force by force—we may justly say: "O miserable England!"

'If Parker and Mutam took Campeach and other places in the Honduras, seated in the heart of the Spanish Indies; burnt towns, killed the Spaniards; and had nothing said to them at their return—and that I myself forebore to look into the Indies, because I would not offend—I may as justly say: "O miserable Sir Walter Raleigh!"

'If I had spent my poor estate, lost my son, suffered by sickness and otherwise a world of miseries: if I had resisted with the manifest hazard of my life the rebels and spoils which my companies would have made; if when I was poor I could have made myself rich; if when I had gotten my liberty, which all men and Nature itself doth so much prize, I voluntarily lost it; if, when I was master of my life, I rendered it again; if, though I might elsewhere have sold my ship and goods and put five or six thousand pounds into my purse, I have brought her into England—I beseech Your Majesty to believe that all this I have done because it should not be said to Your Majesty that Your Majesty had given liberty and trust to a man whose end was but the recovery of his liberty, and who had betrayed Your Majesty's trust.'

He wrote also to the Queen, who, mortally ill at Hampton Court, still pleaded for him with the King who neglected and disliked her. Anne of Denmark was no Elizabeth, yet at this moment she rose to a height of which even Elizabeth might have been proud. Realizing that she herself could do nothing, she abased herself to write to the Favourite Buckingham: 'If I have any power of credit with you, I pray you let me have a trial of it at this time in dealing sincerely and earnestly with the King that Sir Walter Raleigh's life may not be called in question'—a sentence which may stand as an epitome of the degradation of James's court. And in his poem to her, Raleigh coupled her with the great Queen in a verse which, taken out of its context, may seem flattery but which, in those circumstances, was nothing less than justice.

> *O had Truth power, the guiltless could not fall,*
>   *Malice win glory, or Revenge triumph.*
> *But Truth alone cannot encounter all!*

> *Mercy is fled to God, Which Mercy made;*
>   *Compassion dead; Faith turned to Policy.*
> *Friends know not those who sit in Sorrow's shade.*

THE TOWER ONCE MORE

For what we sometime were, we are no more;
  Fortune hath changed our shape, and Destiny
Defaced the very form we had before.

All love and all desert of former times,
  Malice hath covered from my Sovereign's eyes,
And largely laid abroad supposéd crimes. . . .

If I have sold my duty, sold my faith,
  To strangers—which was only due to one—
Nothing I should esteem so dear as death.

But if both God and Time shall make you know
  That I, your humblest vassal, am opprest,
Then cast your eyes on undeservéd woe!

That I and mine may never mourn the miss
  Of Her we had, but praise our living Queen
Who brings us equal, if not greater, bliss.

Not only the English Queen but the French king took
up Raleigh's cause. When the Government, in desperation to find some charge that was not patently ridiculous,
examined members of the French Embassy on the subject
of Raleigh's attempted escape to France, the French
Government suspended diplomatic negotiations and
openly asserted that Raleigh was in prison 'to content the
Spaniards'.

This undoubted truth was the reason why, by some
means or other, he must be killed. His death sentence was,
in fact, pronounced in Madrid the day after he entered

the Tower. On August 11th, Philip of Spain held a Council of State at which it was formally decided that 'the pirate' should, after all, be executed in England.

CHAPTER THIRTY-SIX

THE COUNCIL

The Spanish orders did not reach James until October 15th and they were not carried out for a fortnight, since some legal pretext for the execution had to be found. On October 18th, Sir Edward Coke drew up an advisory document for the King. The difficulty, he pointed out, was that, in law, Sir Walter Raleigh was already dead, as the attainder at Winchester had never been reversed. In these circumstances there were two courses open. One was that with the warrant for Raleigh's execution there should be issued a printed account of his 'late crimes and offences' because of the 'great effluxion of time since his attainder'. The other was that there should be a hearing (which must not be construed as a legal trial) before the Judges, the Privy Council and a selected number of Commissioners, in which the prisoner should be denounced for his recent enormities and then delivered to death.

The second suggestion filled James with alarm. 'We think it not fit', he wrote, 'because it would make him too popular, as was found by experiment at the arraignment at Winchester, where by his wit he turned the hatred of men into compassion for him.' On the other hand, the first course was, in the circumstances, slightly too summary. He suggested a compromise. Raleigh should be brought before the Lords of the Council, should be told of his crimes and then be informed that the judgment given against him in 1603 was at last to be carried out. The paradox of executing him on the charge that he had conspired with Spain against England, if it occurred to James at all, was dismissed in the interests of necessity.

So, on October 22nd, Raleigh was summoned to judgment. The Attorney-General, Yelverton, expatiated on his faults committed before the last voyage, the faults committed during it and the faults committed after it, and told the prisoner that 'never had subject been so obliged to his sovereign' as he had been. The Solicitor-General, Coventry, followed, stressing his feigned illness at Salisbury, his attempted flight, his alleged effort to corrupt the incorruptible Stukeley. Raleigh did not trouble to reply to the specific charges, but contemptuously reminded the Council that the King himself did not, in fact, believe him guilty of treason in 1603, since, if he had, he would certainly not have allowed him to sail to Guiana, well armed, in 1617. He admitted that he had indeed feigned illness, but quoted as a precedent King David, who in danger of his life pretended madness to escape his enemies. He pointed out that he made no attempt to escape until after the King had refused to see him at Salisbury, when he realized at last that 'his confidence in the King' had been 'deceived'. When he was faced with two of his captains who had deserted him in the final stages of his voyage home and who swore that he had 'proposed the taking of the Mexico fleet if the mine failed' he admitted that he had said it but that, so far from having attempted it, he had risked a mutiny among his men by refusing to do it.

Francis Bacon, who for his subservience to James had

that year been made Lord Chancellor, told him he must die.

Two days later Raleigh was brought before the Council once more to hear officially the legal reason for his death, the enforcement of the sentence of 1603. His request that he should be beheaded, not hanged and disembowelled, was granted.

On October 28th, early in the morning, he was taken to the bar of the King's Bench to hear the sentence. He had been ill during the whole of his imprisonment and, during the last few days, had a fever which made him tremble with weakness. Consequently, he had grown careless of his appearance to an extent that made even Wilson remonstrate with him and urge him to have a barber for his hair.

He retorted: 'I must first know who is to have my locks.' If it was the executioner, why should he trouble? And when, at the door of his cell, he met his old valet, Peter, who was genuinely distressed at his untidiness, he made the same answer: 'Dost know, Peter, of any plaster that will set a man's head on again when it is off?'

In court, the Attorney-General reminded those present that Raleigh had already been sentenced to death but that the King 'of his abundant grace' had 'been pleased to show mercy upon him till now'. But now 'justice calls unto him for execution'. But Yelverton was not Coke, and he could not forbear saying: 'Sir Walter Raleigh hath been a statesman and a man who in regard of his parts and quality is to be pitied. He hath been a star at which the world hath gazed. But stars may fall, nay, they must fall when they trouble the sphere wherein they abide.'

The Lord Chief Justice also, Montague, addressed Raleigh in terms which were—and were probably meant to be—a contradiction of the abuse which the cut-purse Popham (eleven years dead) had uttered in 1603: 'Your faith hath hitherto been questioned,' he said; 'however, I am resolved you are a good Christian, for *The History of the World*, which is an admirable work, doth testify as much.' Nevertheless he pointed out to Raleigh, when he attempted to justify his recent conduct, that this was irrelevant since it was under the sentence of 1603 that he was dying. He was then 'justly convicted', and during the past fifteen years, 'might at any minute have been cut off'.

The execution was appointed for the following day, October 29th. The King had chosen this with some care, as it was the day of the Lord Mayor's Show, which he hoped would provide an effective counter-attraction to Londoners.

After sentence, Raleigh was taken to spend his last night in the Gate House at Westminster, which was convenient for the scaffold which was to be prepared 'at or within our Palace of Westminster'. As Raleigh crossed Palace Yard he met an old friend whom he asked whether he would be present next morning. On being told that he hoped to be, Raleigh answered with a smile: 'I do not know what you may do for a place. For mine own part I am sure of one. You must make what shift you can.'

CHAPTER THIRTY-SEVEN

THE LAST NIGHT

That evening the last hope failed. James ignored a petition drawn up in the name of Raleigh's surviving son, Carew—now thirteen—begging for the life 'of my poor father, sometime honoured with many great places of command by the most worthy Queen Elizabeth, the possessor whereof she left him at her death, as a token of her good will to his loyalty'. It was not, perhaps, tactful, but it was Raleigh the Elizabethan who was dying.

Friends who came to take their farewell of him 'found him lifted above the need of comfort to an exaltation of courage which seemed improper'.

'Do not carry it with too much bravery,' said one of them. 'Your enemies will take exception if you do.'

'Do not grudge it to me,' said Raleigh. 'When I come to the sad parting you will see me grave enough.'

The Dean of Westminster, Chaplain to the King and a careful careerist twenty-five years Raleigh's junior,[1] who was sent to prepare him for death, was shocked. 'When I began to encourage him against the fear of death', he recorded, 'he seemed to make so light of it that I wondered at him; and when I told him that the dear servants of God, in better causes than his, had shrunk back and

---

[1] He was made, needless to say, a bishop.

trembled a little, he denied not, yet gave God thanks he never feared death . . . and had rather die so than of a burning fever; with much more to that purpose, with such confidence and cheerfulness, that I was fain to divert my speech another way and wished him not to flatter himself.'

Even when Lady Raleigh came, his courage did not fail. He tried to divert her mind from the inevitable morning by talking of practical things—the vindication of his name, the education of Carew. Almost incoherent, she managed to tell him that she had been granted one favour—the right to dispose of his body.

'It is well, dear Bess,' he said, 'that thou mayest dispose of that dead which thou hadst not always the disposal of when alive.' As midnight struck by the Abbey clock she was taken away from him.

Left alone, he turned to his Bible. What he read we do not know, but we know what he wrote. On the fly-leaf he copied out that poem which he had written, that infinity of years ago, when Essex had arrived at Court to eclipse him:

> *Even such is Time, which takes in trust*
> *Our youth, our joys, and all we have,*
> *And pays us but with age and dust:*
> *Who in the dark and silent grave,*
> *When we have wandered all our ways,*
> *Shuts up the story of our days.*

But he added two lines to it:

> *But from that earth, that grave, that dust,*
> *The Lord shall raise me up, I trust.*

CHAPTER THIRTY-EIGHT

THE SCAFFOLD

The execution had been appointed for eight o'clock —an hour after sunrise. But James's hope that 'the pageants and fine shows might draw away the people from beholding the tragedy of one of the gallant-est worthies that ever England bred' was not realized. Old Palace Yard was so crowded that the procession from the Gate House had some difficulty in passing to the scaffold. Every window was crowded. And all, whether nobles on horseback or citizens on foot, were swept by pity and admiration.

Raleigh had eaten a good breakfast and afterwards smoked a last pipe, making 'no more of death than if it had been to take a journey'. At the scaffold they offered him a cup of sack, which he accepted. Asked whether it was to his liking, he said: 'I will answer you as did the fellow who drank of St. Giles's bowl as he went to Tyburn: "It is a good drink if a man might but tarry by it." ' Near him he noticed an old, bald-headed man, who was being pushed by the guards. He asked him why he had come out on such a bitter morning and what he wanted.

'Nothing but to see you and pray God to have mercy on your soul,' the old man replied.

Raleigh thanked him and gave him his lace night-cap, 'for thou hast more need of it now, friend, than I'.

On the scaffold itself Raleigh prepared to make his

dying speech, exonerating himself for the last time and for the sake of posterity from the charges against him. He apologized for his weakness, in body and voice. But 'this is the third day of my fever; and if I show any weakness, I beseech you to attribute it to my malady, for this is the hour I look for it'.

But, though he strained his voice to the utmost, he could not be heard well by the Lords Arundel and Doncaster, who were on the balcony of a house near by. Arundel called out: 'We will come upon the scaffold', and they moved down to be near him there.

It was to Arundel, after he had set forth his defence, that he appealed for confirmation of his honesty. 'Being in the Gallery in my ship at my departure', he said, 'your Honour took me by the hand and said you would request me one thing, that was: That whether I made a good voyage or bad, yet i should return unto England; when I made a promise and gave you my faith that I would.

'And so you did!' answered Arundel loudly. 'It is true.'

There was one other slander that Raleigh felt he must dispose of. It had been continually repeated that when Essex was on the scaffold he had stood in full view, at one of the Tower windows, smoking and 'puffing out tobacco in disdain of him'. As a matter of fact, he had been in the Armoury, where Essex could not see him, and had often regretted that he had not stayed at the scaffold 'for I heard he had a desire to see me and be reconciled with me'. As for his own feelings for Essex: 'I confess I was of a contrary faction, but I knew that my Lord of Essex was a noble gentleman and that it would be worse with me when he was gone. For those that set me up against him did afterwards set themselves against me.'

THE SCAFFOLD

Of the King he said little—'What have I to do with kings who am about to go before the King of kings?'—and if there was still a bitterness in his reference to Stukeley, he managed to say at the end of him: 'I desire God to forgive him, as I hope to be forgiven.'

There was much, he knew, that he had to be forgiven. He asked all those there to 'join with me in prayer to that great God of Heaven whom I have grievously offended, being a man full of all vanity, who has lived a sinful life in such callings as have been most inducing to it. Of a long time, my course was a course of vanity. I have been a seafaring man, a soldier and a courtier, and in the temptations of the least of these there is enough to overthrow a good mind and a good man.'

The scaffold was cleared of all but Raleigh, the chaplain and the executioner. Raleigh took off his hat and gown and doublet with a composure so complete that one spectator noted: 'He seemed as free from all manner of apprehension, as if he had come hither rather to be a spectator than a sufferer.' He insisted on handling the axe and feeling its edge. 'This is a sharp medicine,' he said, 'but it is a physician for all diseases.'

The executioner threw down his own cloak for Raleigh to kneel on, then himself fell on his knees to beg his forgiveness. Raleigh, placing both hands on his shoulders, gave it willingly and tried to comfort him. 'When I stretch forth both my hands', he said, 'despatch me.'

The chaplain suggested that it would be more seemly if he faced the east. 'It is no matter which way the head lies,' said Raleigh, 'so the heart be right', and put his head on the block. After a few moments of prayer he stretched out his hands.

But the executioner was unnerved and did not strike. Raleigh stretched out his hands again, but again the executioner could not bring himself to deliver the blow. Then Raleigh gave his last command: 'What dost thou fear? Strike, man, strike!'

The head was severed after two blows, as the crowd groaned in execration.

Among the crowd was a young Cornishman, John Eliot, a friend of Buckingham. That day's work eventually changed his allegiance and he became the inspirer of the revolution against the Stuarts, left to die, by the order of James's son, in Raleigh's old cell in the Tower. He left on record his memory of that October morning in 1618.

'All preparations that are terrible were presented to his eye. Guards and officers were about him, the scaffold and the executioner, the axe and the more cruel expectation of his enemies. And what did all this work on the resolution of our Raleigh? made it an impression of weak fear, to distract his reason? Nothing so little did that great soul suffer. His mind became the clearer, as if already it had been freed from the cloud and oppression of the body. Such was his unmoved courage and placid temper that, while it changed the affection of his enemies who had come to witness it and turned their joy to sorrow, it filled all men else with emotion and admiration, leaving with them only this doubt—whether death were more accepable to him or he more welcome unto Death.'

But a shorter sentence may stand as his epitaph. When the executioner held up the head for all to see, an unknown voice from the crowd, topping the tumult, called out: 'We have not such another head to be cut off.'

INDEX

INDEX

INDEX

DATE DUE

SE 24 '85			
OC 7 '85			
OC 21 '85			
Nov 4 '85			
NOV 18 '85			
F			
SEP 25 '86			

PRINTED IN U.S.A.